# The Naturally Frugal Baby

Financial survival strategies and tactics for having a baby without going broke

Peggy Wilson

Second edition published via Lulu.com, January 2011

ISBN:  978-0-578-07836-6

# Table of Contents

## 0

## 1

# 2

# 3

# 4

## Big Things II — Diapering.................................................87

# 5

## Big Things III and IV — Daycare and Health Insurance

# 6

## Baby Equipment and Supplies

# 7

## When the Baby Comes................................................153

# 8

## The Growing Baby.....................................................159

# O

# Introduction: The Real Cost of Having a Baby

Having a baby can be very expensive, according to the experts, but perhaps babies are not as expensive as we have been led to believe.

## *The story of the young couple*

My motivation for writing this book started with an article that I read online. (I can't find the article now, unfortunately.) The story was about a young couple, living in the Pacific Northwest, who were shocked to learn that they really couldn't afford to have a baby yet.

Both the husband and the wife were working; together they made over $70,000 a year. That is not a low household income, so what was the problem? First, they had bought a three-bedroom house at the height of the housing boom, and were fixing it up a little. They also had tens of thousands of dollars of student loan debt, and thousands more dollars of credit card debt. Probably a car loan as well, maybe two; I can't remember. They lived in an area of the country that has a fairly high cost of living.

Their big surprise came when they were told that having a baby would cost them over *$13,000* for the first year alone, not counting prenatal care and birth costs. ($13,000 is the number I remember; the actual number may have been even higher.) And this estimate came from the United States Department of Agriculture, so no one questioned it.

I had seen articles before about USDA estimates that raising a child from birth to age eighteen will cost around $200,000, but I had a very hard time believing that an infant could cost $13,000 per year. For that much money, you could just about send them off to college. So I did some digging, and learned more about how the USDA came up with that number.

## The cost for baby's first year, according to the USDA

The $13,000 estimate apparently came from the USDA's Cost of Raising a Child calculator.[1] Its stated purpose is to "estimate how much it will annually cost to raise a child". The calculator is based on a report, *Expenditures on Children by Families 2007,*[2] about what families across the nation actually spent on raising their children. The report was based on the data from older surveys, such as the 1990-92 *Consumer Expenditure Survey* and the 1987 *Health Care Survey*, with costs adjusted to 2007 dollars.

The Cost of Raising a Child Calculator computes the annual cost of raising children based on marital status, family size, ages of children, family income, and geographical area. So I did a calculation for my own family—a family of four with a two-year-old and an infant, living in the urban or suburban Midwest with an annual income less than $45,100—and this[3] is what I got for the USDA's estimate of our annual costs:

- Housing: $5000
- Food: $1920
- Transportation: $1680
- Clothing (including diapers): $600
- Health: $1120
- Childcare and Education: $2380
- Other: $1260
- Total $13960 (national average $15660).

---

1 The Cost of Raising a Child Calculator can be found at
**http://www.cnpp.usda.gov/calculatorintro.htm**
2 The *Expenditures on Children by Families 2007* report is available online at
**http://www.cnpp.usda.gov/Publications/CRC/crc2007.pdf**
3 In the summer of 2009; the calculator has since been updated.

Whoa there—that's almost $14,000, and nearly a third of our gross annual income! How did we afford to have children in the first place? How could two small children be costing us so much?

Then I did the math for myself, and calculated our *actual* expenses for the year:

- Housing: $1570 for a larger apartment, with one additional bedroom, plus about $170 in extra laundry (i.e., utility) costs.

- Food: $520 including extra food for me as a nursing mother.

- Transportation: $100 at most (sitting in the idling car with sleeping children), but with children we made fewer trips; car seats cost us about $100 per year (amortized).

- Clothing: $580 including diapers—both cloth and disposables.

- Health: currently about $3400 with a high-deductible health plan.

- Childcare and Education: $0, since I stay at home.

- Other: $160 for staying in a motel on trips to visit family, instead of driving straight through (but we take fewer trips overall now); I left out the little things that we buy for our kids, because we pay for those by reallocating money that we would have spent on little things for ourselves, so there is no real additional cost.

- Total: $6600.

That's only one-half of the national average! The USDA calculator was too high in almost every category.

Well, let's dig a little deeper into the details of the calculator. What does it include? And, more importantly, what does it leave out? **(If you don't want to wade through all the gory details, skip ahead to page 22.)**

**Housing:** Many people buy a house around the time that they start a family; this drives up the average housing cost. The USDA figured cost of housing (and transportation and miscellaneous) on a per capita basis—by dividing the total family cost by the number of family members. They had reasons, explained in the depths of the report, for doing it that way, but it overstates the actual cost of housing an infant.

I had better data and was able to calculate the marginal cost for my family—the actual additional costs incurred from housing our children. We are currently renting a three bedroom apartment; if we did not have children we would be renting a two bedroom unit (using one bedroom as an office), so I figured our additional housing expenses as the difference between the two.[4] Plus, of course, the additional utility costs of the laundry generated by the children, which includes washing cloth diapers and wipes. If I figured housing costs on a per capita basis, it would be $6700 per year for two children, which is just silly.

**Food:** The USDA's Center for Nutrition Policy and Promotion tracks food costs for food plans at four cost levels. My family's budget is closest to the "Thrifty Plan".[5] I breastfeed, which requires a little more food for me, but saves a bundle on formula. I also don't buy special baby food.

**Transportation:** Many people buy larger cars, minivans, or SUVs to transport their families. We are still driving our old car, but would have to buy a bigger vehicle to accommodate a third child and car seat. So our primary additional transportation cost for our children is that of extra idling— sitting in the car to not wake the children sleeping in their car seats. We do much less driving now that we have children. (Really, our children are saving us money in this category.) Car seats expire after five or six years, so I figure our car seats, amortized, cost us about $100/year.

The USDA also used per capita cost for this category: total transportation costs for the household, divided by the number of family members. On this basis, my family's transportation costs for both children would be about $1800.

**Clothing:** The USDA includes diapers in this category. Our clothing costs are mainly for diapers and shoes. Nearly all of our children's clothing so far has been gifts, thrift store finds, or hand-me-downs. We have used both disposable and cloth diapers,

---

4 Some leases or local ordinances limit the number of persons that can occupy an apartment. A new baby may or may not count toward the limit. With two children, we would probably have to rent at least a two-bedroom apartment.

5 The Center for Nutrition Policy and Promotion does not have a useful, succinct summary of the different food plans on their website. The "Thrifty Plan" is their lowest-cost plan for meeting nutritional needs.

but our cloth diaper costs at this point are only for laundering them, which is included in the Housing category.

**Health:** The health care cost estimates are based on the 1987 *National Medical Expenditure Survey*, adjusted for inflation, while health care expenditures have generally been rising faster than inflation since that time. So this is one area where the USDA calculator will tend to severely underestimate. The calculator does not include the cost of prenatal care, or of labor and delivery services. These can vary widely, and insurance coverage for maternity care also varies widely.

We pay about $3400 a year for two children for health insurance premiums. They are both quite healthy, so really no additional costs there (except for infrequent urgent care visits).

**Childcare and Education:** The USDA includes cost of daycare, and other educational expenses. I stay at home, and we don't use babysitters other than Grandma, so no expense there. Also, we are spending basically zero on education at this age. We do read a lot, but mostly used books, gifted books, and library books. The USDA's 2007 report noted that about 50% of families use commercial daycare.

**Other:** Gifts for the children; getting a motel to spread a twelve-hour drive to visit family over two days (but this is counterbalanced by less frequent visits). These things are paid for with money that we used to spend on ourselves, that we now spend on our children.

So what else is being left out? Well, the tax advantages of having dependents, for one thing. Just the child tax credit of $1000 per child is offsetting almost one-third of what our children cost. Given our income level and family size, we probably qualify for government aid programs that we are not taking advantage of. (The calculator does not include any government aid in income, and thus underestimates spending on children of the lowest-income families.)

The way that the USDA calculated housing and transportation costs is rather unrealistic. Calculating these on a strictly per capita basis assumes that each family member uses these resources equally, which is unlikely to be true.

The USDA also does not consider substitution effects—where the parents spend less in other areas in order to spend more on their children. Overall, their estimate tends to be an overestimate, except in Health Care, and in Childcare and Education for families that use daycare.

Altogether, I figure that my two children cost us about $3300 a year (each) once they are born, and that is not extra money that we need to earn—we cover it just by changing our old spending patterns. Our income has not risen since we started a family; in fact, it has dropped considerably, but we are making it go a lot farther than it used to. The old saying was "Two can live as cheaply as one"—meaning that a married couple could get along on the same income as a single person. With us, four can live as cheaply as two. Granted, they are still little, and will cost somewhat more when they are older; the U.S. averages in the 2009 report show that that an older teenager costs about $1000 more per year than a toddler for the lower income bracket, about $2000 more per year for the middle bracket, and about $4000 more per year for the upper bracket. However, family income also tends to increase over time.

I had even more fun when I gave us a fictional three-year-old and recomputed: the estimated cost of three children would be $16,286 (national average $18,234), add a four-year-old and the cost would be: $21,822 ($24,409).[6] The first two children "cost" $14,000; the third child would "cost" an additional $2300; the fourth child would "cost" $5500. This estimated cost per additional child is not exactly linear! The 2007 report notes[7]: "Families will spend more or less on a child depending on the number of other children in the household and economies of scale."

In short, here are the reasons that the USDA analysis is off for my family:

- ◆ **Accounting.** The USDA figured some costs in a different way than I did— usually overestimating.
- ◆ **Outdated data.** Particularly for health care costs.
- ◆ **Frugality.** Things that we spend less money on than the average family does. Childcare, food, educational stuff.

---

6 Calculated in the summer of 2009.

7 Page 6.

Since the USDA estimate was so far off for my family, maybe there is some hope for the young couple in the article to be able to afford to start a family. Here are some more reasons why I think they should take a deep breath and relax:

- They are already paying the Housing and Transportation portions of the cost estimate; about a third of the total cost.

- Their household income landed them in the USDA's highest income (and highest spending) bracket. While the USDA can tell them what other higher-income families spend, that's not what they necessarily *have* to spend.

- They are young, and have time to get their finances under control before the biological clock runs out.

Unfortunately, there are also reasons why they should keep panicking a little:

- They have way too much debt, overall.

- They bought too much house for their total income. With the housing crash, they will probably have a very difficult time selling the house to move somewhere more affordable. The house that they bought as a place to start their family may be, ironically, their main obstacle to starting a family.

- They will have to both keep working full-time to keep up with their bills, and so will have to pay for daycare (the costs of which the USDA helpfully underestimated, by including parents who don't use daycare in computing the average). This will eat up about half of an after-tax income for them.

- If either of them loses their job, they will be struggling to keep afloat, even without children.

- By the time they get on a better financial footing, they will be into their thirties, at least.

My purpose in writing this book is to help others keep from making the same mistakes that the young couple in the article did. Or, if it's too late for that, then I hope to at least point out some ways of getting out of the financial quagmire more quickly.

Before you try out the Cost of Raising a Child Calculator yourself, read on to see what changes have been made in the latest versions.

## *Changes in the methodology of calculating the cost of raising a child*

Since I wrote the above sections, the 2008 and 2009 *Expenditures on Children by Families* reports[8] have been released, and the Cost of Raising a Child Calculator has been updated.[9] The USDA has made a number of changes to their methodology of determining how much children cost. Here are some things about the methodology and assumptions to note:

- Clothing expenditures (which include dry-cleaning costs!) are assumed to be evenly spread across children.

- Cost of daycare is now only calculated based on families that use it. Previously, it was calculated based on all families; about half of families use family members for daycare, or no daycare at all. Cost of daycare does include families who use it part-time, which tends to lower the average cost.

- For the 2009 report, the data sources include the 2005-6 *Consumer Expenditure Survey* (adjusted to 2009 dollars) and the USDA's 2008 Food Plans.

- Health care expenses are now based on the 2005 *Medical Expenditure Panel Survey*, which is a nice change, since previously the USDA was using data from *1987*, adjusted for inflation, while health care expenditures increased faster than inflation for twenty years. (However, for some reason health care expenses as given in the latest report have not changed for my family; they are *exactly* the same as before.)

- Transportation costs now include only family-related transportation, about 60% of total household transportation, but beyond that are still calculated on a per capita basis. They do not include the costs of buying a larger or more reliable vehicle.

- Miscellaneous/Other costs are calculated purely on a per capita basis, and include personal care, entertainment, and reading expenses.

---

8 The source of the data for the Cost of Raising a Child Calculator.

9 I reran the calculator (in December 2010), with the same inputs as before, and the results were: Housing $5680, Food $2100, Transportation $1860, Clothing $1220, Health $1120, Childcare and Education $3980, Other $940, and Total $16,900.

◆ Housing costs now include the average cost of an additional bedroom for each child, in place of the per capita calculation used in earlier years. It does not include the costs of living in a better school district, or of extra household space for children, such as yards, playrooms, or family rooms.

◆ The USDA calculations assume a two-child family ; one-child families, where parents tend to spend more on the child, and three-or-more children families, where parents tend to spend less per child, are accounted for by scaling factors.

◆ Larger families generally share more rooms, hand down more clothes, buy in family-sized quantities, ride together more, and receive more sibling discounts.

◆ The USDA assumes that people stay in the same income group over time. This is a big assumption; I have been in four of the five income quintiles myself, in the last ten years. Most people move into higher income groups with age, although some people (households, actually) may move down.[10]

◆ The analysis does not include prenatal care, any costs after age seventeen, cost of life insurance for parents, government spending on children such as Medicaid and subsidized school lunches, spending on children by other relatives, opportunity costs for parents (the things parents give up for the sake of their children), or substitution effects (where parents spend less in other areas in order to spend more on their children).

The household income brackets from the 2009 report are: below $56,670, from $56,670 to $98,120, and above $98,120. (For some reason, the brackets in the 2010 online calculator are slightly lower.) These are probably too high, considering the on-going effects of the recession—the Young Couple in the story would now fall in the middle income bracket, instead of the top bracket.

The reports also look back at data from earlier years. Compared to 1960, parents today are spending more on housing, much more on childcare (because so many more mothers work now), and much more on health care (inflation-adjusted spending more than doubled), but less on food and clothing, and slightly less on transportation.

---

10 For more about how income distribution varies, mostly by age and work experience, see Thomas Sowell's excellent *Basic Economics: A Citizen's Guide to Understanding the Economy.*

**The Cost of Raising a Child calculator's main weakness is that it can't really *predict* the costs—it can only give you averages of reported spending from the people in the survey.** So, give it a try sometime, but don't let the numbers discourage you from having a child—it can be done *much* more cheaply.

## *The real cost of having a baby*

"The newborn baby has only three demands. They are warmth in the arms of its mother, food from her breast, and security in the knowledge of her presence."—Grantly Dick Read[11]

What does a little baby really need? Not much, actually. Just the loving presence of their mother. And that happens to be exactly what little babies want. If you could decipher their cries, you'd hear them saying things like: "I'm too little to be left alone!" "I want my mother!" "I'm hungry, where's the boob?"

Cave babies had little more than the loving presence of their mother. Jesus Christ as a baby had little more than this (see sidebar). To a little baby, Mother is the only essential.

The biggest cost of having a baby is not formula, or diapers, or daycare, or health insurance, or even sending them to college. It is opportunity cost—the opportunities that you give up the chance to pursue when you have a baby.

> **The Baby Jesus Test**
>
> Jesus Christ was born under very humble circumstances, and grew up in a rather poor family. The "Baby Jesus Test" is: **Did Jesus have this as a baby?** It is a way of separating wants and what I call "social needs" from true physical needs.

The opportunity to work long hours and build up career experience and earning power. The opportunity to save aggressively for retirement, and to earn enough Social Security credits to qualify for full retirement benefits.[12] The opportunity to casually go out in the evening or away for the weekend.

But these losses should be balanced against the opportunities gained: seeing the first smile, the first step, the first day of school. Passing on your values to the next genera-

---

11 Quoted in *The Joy of Being a Woman*, page 103.

12 If you believe that Social Security will still be around by the time that you retire. I'm not counting on it.

tion, which maximizes your impact on the future. Preserving your cultural heritage. Stretching your growth as a person in ways you never imagined.

Our society disregards the substantial benefits of a mother's care—including the benefits of living in harmony with her maternal instincts, and of enjoying the hormonal rewards of a close relationship with her baby. Even fathers are kept too much separated from their children by the demands of modern work and culture.

I urge you to not put off having children for too long. The biological clock is indeed ticking: fertility in women generally declines fairly steadily with age, while infertility increases. Fertility treatments are invasive and expensive. Older mothers also have somewhat higher risks of miscarriage and pregnancy complications, not to mention birth defects. These can greatly increase the cost of having a baby. Adoptions are also lengthy, expensive processes (even if you can take the adoption tax credit).

On the other hand don't have children too early, either! Taking on the responsibility of caring for a baby when you can't even take care of yourselves is not a good idea.

## *Purpose of the book*

The purpose of this book is to help you afford to have a baby and to help you survive the baby's first year financially. Too many people think that they can't afford to have a baby, or to have another baby. But a society that makes reproduction unaffordable is a society that is headed for extinction. The divine mandate found in Genesis Chapter 9, Verse 1 implies that resources for procreation will not be lacking: "Be fruitful and multiply, and fill the earth" (RSV). Even if you're not motivated by religion to reproduce, it is a matter of practical evolution—survival of the fittest, in this case the financially and economically fittest. If you're not financially fit yet, it is not too late to change.

I will give you strategies and tips for arranging your life to be frugal and to be able to afford having a baby in the first place, as well as some ideas for how to keep your baby expenditures down. Keep in mind that the goal of frugality is not to be as cheap as possible. Rather, I define frugality as:

*Extending your standard of living by carefully allocating resources away from lesser wants and false "needs", and toward true needs and greater wants.*

I call this "look poorer, but live richer".

For an all-around buying guide, check out *Baby Bargains*, by Denise and Alan Fields, which is an excellent reference for shopping for baby gear, and for finding out which manufacturers and brands have the best reputations. It is currently in its eighth edition. In this book I am not going to tell you how to spend $4000 instead of $7000 on baby stuff[13]; I am going to tell you how you can avoid spending money at all, or at least how you can spend much, much less.

If you need more hard-core frugality in your life, then you should read *The Complete Tightwad Gazette*, by Amy Dacyczyn, which has many hints for having babies on the cheap. She re-equipped herself (for twins!) for only $100.[14]

While my sympathies lie more with the natural-parenting camp than with the parenting mainstream, I can't help but notice that this subculture has its own long list of must-buys for babies, and that most of the recommended items are really unnecessary (and often terribly overpriced). For all the true necessities, there are alternatives that are much more frugal, and just as environmentally and socially conscious.

I am well aware that there are times where frugal strategies just won't work; times of crisis tend to burn through your money, time, and energy all at once. And you can only stretch a dollar so far—sometimes the only reasonable solution is to find a way to boost your income. But it *is* possible to live quite well on incomes that most people would consider "impossible", and learning to use your resources wisely will definitely put you in a better position for weathering future troubles.

## *Organization of the book*

This book is arranged by time: things to think about before getting pregnant, things to do during pregnancy, things to do once the baby arrives, and matters regarding the growing baby. At the end there is a list of references and resources.

---

13 *Baby Bargains*, 8th edition, p. 2: "Industry estimates" for retail-priced baby equipment for the first year: $7040. If you follow the *Baby Bargains* tips: $4149.

14 In circa 1998 dollars, as well as circa 1998 safety standards. There has been even more "safety inflation" than monetary inflation in the past ten years or so.

## A Note

I don't know everything; I learn new things every day. I am not a financial planner, nor am I a doctor, except of philosophy. Some of the ideas in this book are unconventional, based on my own individual experience and opinions, or on the advice of random strangers on the Internet, which I have tested only on my own family. I have written this book in my spare time, with two young children underfoot, so I haven't been able to research or write about everything as extensively as I would have liked to. Do your own reading and research; there is a long list of helpful resources at the end of the book. Use your own good judgment as to which ideas and strategies from this book you should implement, and which you should not. The point of this book is to give you options, not burdens, although it is true that many of the frugal baby care options tend to reinforce each other synergistically.

## A Further Note, about Martians

These are Martians, who will help illustrate some of the absurdities of how Earthlings have and care for babies:

# 1

# Before Getting Pregnant

Your physical health, your financial health, and your spiritual health will each have a large effect on how you start pregnancy and parenthood. You can save yourself a lot of time, money, and trouble later by taking care of these things before you get pregnant.

## *Physical health*

### *Nutrition*

The first thing is to nourish yourself by eating well. Improvements in your diet may cost a few more dollars a week, but it shouldn't be more than that. Eat simpler, less processed, and more nutritious foods. Get outside for fresh air and sunshine, drink enough water, get enough sleep, and so on.

If you're trying to conceive, doctors recommend eating like you're already pregnant. If you drink alcohol, cut way back; giving your baby fetal alcohol syndrome is no good. Cut back on the caffeine, too. Folate (folic acid) is important, to prevent neural tube defects—the time that you critically need it is before you even know that you're pregnant. Folate occurs naturally in foods like beans, peas, green leafy vegetables, broccoli, and many others. The government mandates folic acid fortification in breads and other grain products. Iron, calcium, vitamins A and C, and B vitamins are also important.

Some people recommend starting prenatal vitamins before trying to get pregnant. Inexpensive prenatal vitamins are available over-the-counter, or by prescription. Read the labels to compare inexpensive vitamins against more expensive ones. You can take one enormous pill per day, or several smaller ones. (When I am pregnant, especially when I have morning sickness, choking down one pill a day is enough for me.) There are now chewable prenatal vitamins on the market, but I haven't yet seen them in stores.

Don't worry too much about trying to lose weight before you get pregnant if you are otherwise healthy. Good nutrition is more important at this point. The biggest risk from being overweight during pregnancy is of being overtreated medically.[15]

## *Exercise*

Exercise in moderation is helpful, but don't expect to be able to exercise heavily all the way through pregnancy. You will hit new heights of fatigue in the first and third trimesters. Later in pregnancy, your ligaments loosen up, and you will need to move more carefully. If you're going to exercise anything, work on your upper body strength. Most newborns weigh between five and ten pounds, and they grow very rapidly. They also expect to be carried around all the time. Get your arms, back, shoulders, and core muscles ready for this.

## *Fertility Awareness and Natural Family Planning*

Before pregnancy is also a good time to learn about Fertility Awareness (also called Natural Family Planning). In short, you learn how to identify the symptoms of ovulation, so you can determine when the best times for intercourse are, to maximize your chances of conceiving (or of not conceiving). The symptoms of ovulation include[16]:

- Temperature shift: The woman's waking temperature rises by about half a degree Fahrenheit at ovulation, and stays high for the rest of the cycle, until about the time that menstrual bleeding starts.

- Cervix : Soft and open, and lower in position.

---

15 See the articles at Plus Size Pregnancy for more information: **http://www.plus-size-pregnancy.org/**

16 It's best to find a book or take a class on the subject, to help you get started. One book (that I haven't yet read myself) is *Taking Charge of Your Fertility*, by Toni Weschler.

◆ Midpain: Some women experience a midpain in one side of the abdomen (this is actually ovulation pain, at the ovary).

◆ Cervical mucus: Mucus which is clear and stretchy like egg white.

Having a well-charted cycle can help to give you a more accurate due date, or even help identify physical problems that are interfering with getting and staying pregnant.

When you can more or less predict the day of ovulation, and you combine that with the facts that sperm can live up to about six days, and that an egg is good for not much more than a day, you can determine which days are potentially fertile and which are not.

When it is used for preventing pregnancy, the fertility awareness/symptothermal method is about 98% effective; most "failures" are failures to abstain rather than failures to determine fertile days. It is very empowering to understand what is going on in your body. When I first encountered natural family planning (in reading *The Joy of Being a Woman*, by Ingrid Trobisch), I was struck by its simplicity and elegance, and I was quite angry that I didn't learn about it until I was well into my twenties.

### *Health problems and stress*

Existing health problems that can affect pregnancy should be addressed. Many sexually transmitted diseases can adversely affect a pregnancy, and should be treated (if possible) beforehand. Diabetes is another big problem in pregnancy. Physical issues such as a bad back should be addressed if possible. Finally, try to cut back on sources of stress. Having a baby is stressful enough!

## *Financial Health*

I have not yet read *Your Money: The Missing Manual*, by J.D. Roth, but it should be a good basic resource for getting your finances into shape. Many couples neglect this area until after children are born, but it is much easier if you tackle it ahead of time. Having children tends to severely slow the rate at which you can get ahead financially (as noted by Amy Dacyczyn in *The Complete Tightwad Gazette*), even if you've made all the right choices up to that point.

## Getting married

Are you married yet?  Probably you should be—marriage is the number one way to keep mothers and children out of poverty.[17]  Even Baby Jesus grew up with two parents living under the same roof.  But don't get married to the wrong person...divorce tends to be financially (not to mention emotionally) devastating.  Even marrying someone who is paying child support for prior children can make for a huge financial challenge.  *Your choice of marriage partner is the single most important economic decision that you will ever make.*

Premarital counseling can help you both face the hard questions about finances and how you plan to deal with them as a couple.  Many pastors and churches provide free premarital counseling, as part of their ministry to the community.  Some couples never do fully unite their finances, but I think this is a mistake.

## Credit cards and debit cards

Many people have found that credit cards are an incredibly convenient way of running up huge debts.  My advice is to live without them as much as you can.  They are just a big scam.  Even if you pay them off every month, and regularly collect "rewards", odds are that sooner or later you will run into a stretch where money is tight, and then build up a balance with substantial interest, fees, charges, and penalties tacked on, and it will be very difficult to pay off.  I get scared off from credit cards every time I start reading the fine print on a credit card offer, because I can see that the game is rigged, and not in the consumer's favor.

Some credit card companies are now watching their customers' spending patterns (purchases and places of purchase) very carefully, and yanking back credit lines—or jacking up interest rates—when the customer seems to be buying in a state of financial

---

17 The *Expenditures on Children by Families* 2008 report says that single-parent households spend only five or six hundred dollars less, per child and per year, than two-parent households, but it also says that the average income for a single-parent household ($25,220) is much lower than that of a two-parent household ($36,380) .  The single parent income figures also do not include child support, or any other support provided by the other parent.  In any case, the single parent category mostly consists of parents who were once married.

distress. So even if you have access to credit now, you might not have it when you really need it.

The Credit Card Accountability Responsibility and Disclosure Act of 2009 will not be a panacea for credit card woes. Many companies raised interest rates and fees before the law took effect, even on their most responsible cardholders.

Some people claim that is impossible nowadays to live without a credit card. It is not impossible; not yet. This is how we handle large and emergency expenses without using a credit card:

1. Have savings in liquid form—a bank account or cash. (Dave Ramsey recommends starting with a baby Emergency Fund of $1000, before making a serious effort to pay down debt.)

2. Pay by cash, or by check, moving money from savings if necessary.

3. If the amount is too much to pay off immediately by check and drawing on savings, work out a payment plan. Even if your creditor charges interest, they are unlikely to charge as much interest as a credit card company would.

4. In some cases, searching for a more affordable option may be your only choice.

Some people use their credit cards to make purchases or book travel for their work. But really, you should be entrusted with a company credit card, if these tasks are necessary for your job. Otherwise, you are making small loans to your employers, while taking on the risk of not being paid back in a timely manner, and of incurring interest charges. If you have no choice, I suggest keeping one card exclusively for business use, and being extremely diligent about saving receipts and getting prompt reimbursement.

For our infrequent travel or online purchases, we use a debit card. (This account is separate from our main checking account.) Even a debit card has problems; it is far too easy to lose track of debit card purchases—and automatic payments, and fees, and holds placed by retailers—and end up with multiple overdraft charges. (This is another scam, in my opinion, but it is how banks make most of their money these days. Eventually, the most irresponsible account holders end up on the bankers' blacklist, unable to open a new account anywhere.)

It is not easy to rent a car with a debit card these days, but it is still possible.

Electronic forms of payment are generally more trouble to keep track of than they are worth. Stick with payment methods that make it easy for you to keep track of what you have, and that don't let you spend more than you have. Keep good records of what you spent where. Tracking every single penny you spend is not a bad idea.

## Paying off debt

You can greatly increase your financial fitness to reproduce by getting out of debt. That means paying off whatever debt you have, and then not taking on any new debt. The good news is that the less debt you have, the richer you will be, because you won't be paying interest and fees, thus your real buying power will increase. So will your ability to invest in things that make *you* money. That is how the rich get richer, and the poor get poorer.

Many people have been burying their heads in the sand for a long time, and don't even know how far in debt they are. The first step to getting out of debt is to figure out how deep the hole is. Take a deep breath, make a list, and add it all up.

How to pay off debt? Making only the minimum payments will keep you in debt for far too long. So you will need to pay much more than the minimum. The first thing is to find some spare money—probably by cutting back your spending in some area, or by earning more money in some way. Then apply this money to your debt. (Easier said than done when money is tight, I know.)

Mathematically, the best debt to pay off first is the one with the highest interest rate. But some people start with the smallest debt first, and work their way up to the largest. (Dave Ramsey's Debt Snowball works this way; go read his book. Snowballing means that once you pay off a debt, you start applying the amount that you were paying on it to the next debt that you want to pay off.) I prefer to start with the "most annoying debt"— determine which debt is the most bothersome, and pay that one off first. This gives a quick psychological payoff, and a good start on the right path.

For crushing debts that are impossible to pay off, you can try to settle with your creditors for a reduced amount. Most would prefer that you paid some fraction of your debt, rather than none of it. Get all agreements in writing. Filing for bankruptcy should be reserved for extreme hardship; it isn't nearly as easy as it used to be, and it won't necessarily erase all debt. Federal student loans, for instance, cannot be discharged in bankruptcy. Another extreme measure, for debt secured by collateral, is to default and let the creditor take the collateral. This may or may not be acceptable to your personal system of ethics, and you will probably still owe the difference between the amount of the loan and the value of the collateral. State laws vary on what recourse your creditors have if you default, so check the law before you walk away from a debt. You also need to know whether you will be taxed on any amount that is forgiven by your creditors. Read the fine print in your loan or credit paperwork, and don't hesitate to talk to a lawyer or a tax preparer if you need to.

One way or another, shedding debt is going to affect your credit score, and not necessarily for the better, because one part of your score is your willingness to apply for credit. The details of the various scoring algorithms are kept secret, but remember that credit scoring was created by lenders, for lenders. They want to extend credit and make loans, and they want these to be repaid, eventually. But they also want to make a lot of money in the form of interest and fees. Debts that go unpaid are a loss to them. People that pay off debt too quickly are not as profitable for them as people who pay a little late, and then pay extra in interest and late fees.

I am not a fan of credit scores. The credit card companies and other lenders don't care what I think about their often-sleazy business practices; why should I care what they think about me? Anyway, don't worry too much about how high your credit score is; it only has to be "good enough". A low credit score may cost you more money in some areas: car insurance, loans, background checks for employment or rental housing. But in my opinion, the value of a high credit score is very much overrated.

## *Figuring out your benefits*

While the health care reform bills were passed by Congress last spring, not much has changed yet—a multitude of health plans continue to be available, some private and some public, and one's health insurance is still primarily determined by what is offered (or not offered) by one's employer.

If you are employed, before pregnancy is the time to inquire—discreetly—about your employer's maternity leave policies and what benefits you will get under your health care plan (if any). You should start thinking about whether you want to go back to work after having the baby. I recommend staying at home—usually this is easiest for the whole family, even if it is a big financial sacrifice—but you will have to decide what works best for you and your own family.

This is the time to read your health insurance contract (or statement of coverage or benefits handbook) and see what is covered and what is not. (Especially if, like me, maternity is your first major encounter with the ins and outs of health insurance.) The documents will tell you exactly what is and isn't covered, although not necessarily in a very readable form. Don't just accept what they say on their website, or in any summary of benefits you might have; go right to the source, which is the only legally binding version.

Benefits vary widely, from maternity costs covered 100%, all the way down to 0%, or to the minimum allowed by law in your state, so take a look and see what you have. Prenatal visits may or may not be covered, or they may be considered "office visits", with your regular co-pay. You can expect to get separate bills from the hospital or birth center, from whoever attends your labor (obstetrician, nurse-midwife, or midwife), from an anesthesiologist who administered drugs, and so on. You can also expect to see separate bills for the baby's hospital care—from the hospital and from the doctor who did the newborn exam.

It may help to know that your insurance documents are written in Insurance, not in English, and so they must be translated and interpreted. These are some terms you may encounter:

- Co-pay: amount that you must pay per service. Ask if you will have a co-pay for prenatal visits, and what it will be, because this can add up as you have frequent prenatal visits in late pregnancy.
- Co-insurance: after you pay the deductible amount, the insurance company will pay a certain percentage, and you will pay the rest (80% and 20% are common).

- ◆ Coordination of benefits: how the insurance companies determine which plan will pay what, if you are covered by more than one plan.

- ◆ Customary fee: what the insurance company insists is a fair price for the service, and also usually the most that they will pay for it.

- ◆ Deductible: amount you pay per term (usually annually), before the insurance company will start paying for things. Some services may be exempt from the deductible requirement. The baby, after being born, usually has a separate deductible. One thing to note is that not everything you pay out of pocket may count toward your deductible. Our insurance only counts the "usual and customary" portions of the costs toward our deductible.

- ◆ Exclusions: things that the insurance plan won't pay for, ever.

- ◆ High-deductible health plan: you pay lower premiums, in exchange for a much higher deductible. Can be used in conjunction with a Health Savings Account (HSA).

- ◆ In-network: the insurance company's list of health care providers (preferred providers) that it has payment agreements with.

- ◆ Lifetime maximum: once the insurance company pays this much out in claims for you, they are done. Health care reform is eliminating these for most plans.

- ◆ Open enrollment: the period where you are free to sign up for the insurance plan. Otherwise, you may have to wait for a qualifying event in your life circumstances to enroll. (Being born is a qualifying event, for the baby.)

- ◆ Out-of-network: refers to health care providers that don't have payment agreements with your insurance company. You can expect to pay much more out of pocket if you choose out-of-network providers.

- ◆ Out-of-pocket maximum: the maximum that you have to pay towards deductibles, copays, and other co-insurance; after that the insurance should cover 100% of (the customary fees for) non-excluded services.

- ◆ Pre-existing condition: a condition that you had before the insurance coverage began.

- Primary care physician: your main doctor.

- Provider: health-care provider or facility.

- Provider responsibility: amount that the insurance company will ignore and not bother to pay, because it is more than their customary fee for the service. For out-of-network providers, you will likely have to pay this portion, while in-network providers usually absorb these costs as part of their payment agreement with the insurance plan.

- Waiting period: how long you have to wait for coverage to begin.

Two questions to ask your insurer are: If a pregnancy starts in one calendar year, but ends in another, are you going to have to pay your deductibles twice? Conceiving and giving birth in the same calendar year could save you a lot of money. And, when does the insurance company want to know that the baby has arrived? Some want you to ask them for pre-authorization before you even go to the hospital, others want to know within some number of days after the birth.

Even if your insurance is not so great, don't give up. The very worst case is that you will have to pay everything out of pocket. Somewhere between five and ten thousand dollars altogether for a simple vaginal birth, in the hospital. Perhaps less if you use a certified nurse-midwife (CNM), and/or you take a more natural route. Homebirths with a midwife start at about two or three thousand dollars, but not all states allow midwives to attend homebirths. Unassisted childbirth (with no healthcare provider in attendance) is not necessarily illegal, but it does require parents who choose it to take full responsibility, for everything, and may be grounds for the state to accuse them of medical neglect. Left to nature, most women in their childbearing years will have a baby every two or three years—therefore, what you can afford for a birth should probably be based on what you can save up over two years or so, all things considered.

If even that seems out of reach, then you are very probably poor enough to qualify for some form of government assistance. Medicaid pays for nearly half of the total maternity and newborn hospital charges in the U.S.[18] But I'd consider it only as a last resort.

---

18 Forty-three percent of $86 billion in 2006, according to this Childbirth Connection article: **http://www.childbirthconnection.org/pdfs/maternity-care-in-health-care-reform.pdf**

## *Living on one income and staying at home—things to consider*

Before getting pregnant, scale back your lifestyle so that you can live comfortably on one income, even if you plan to go back to work after maternity leave. Many mothers plan to go back, but once they meet their baby they find themselves very reluctant to leave the baby and return to work. This is quite natural, and is hardwired into the human mother via instincts and hormones, although our culture makes little allowance for it. So plan ahead.

Two full-time jobs per couple do not necessarily lead to financial security. Not when you need two incomes just to pay the mortgage and keep food on the table. (Particularly in a severe recession such as the present one, with very high unemployment rates—the highest in decades—and chronic structural employment problems that will only delay any economic recovery.) A full-time person at home can contribute almost as much as a full-time worker, by attending to the economic efficiency of the household—contributing time to the household instead of money, and insourcing more of the household's work than a two-income couple can. Cleaning, laundry, cooking, childcare, money management, repairs, and so on are quite expensive in money if you have to pay someone else to do them, or in time when you have scarce off-work hours in which to attend to them yourself. Taking this a step further, *Radical Homemakers*, by Shannon Hayes, advocates for restoring the home to a center of production, instead of a center of consumption.

So figure out for yourself what the net value of the second income is, after taxes, work-related expenses, and daycare costs. (Not to mention the opportunity costs of having much less time to deal with things at home.) Divide by the hours worked, and you have the net hourly wage. It is entirely possible to be losing money by working, in the short term.

Watch out for the unexpected costs of staying at home: you will use more utilities and more household supplies, and eat more food while at home. Some stay-at-home mothers develop such a great need to get out of the house that they spend even more time driving than they did when they were commuting. Also, the environment at home matters more when you are there all day, every day. We decided to move to a larger apartment than we strictly needed, just to have enough "places to be" during the day. I spend more time thinking about how things are decorated and arranged, because I am there looking at them all day. There is also more wear and tear on surfaces and furnishings when you are home more. These are little things, but they do add up in the long run.

Any frugal changes in lifestyle that you want to implement—cooking more from scratch, for example—try to start doing them before the baby is born, to get over the learning curve, and to be set for the challenge of doing them with a baby later on.

## Continuing to work; working at home

If both parents are going to be working, it is best to have work hours that are either extremely predictable, or extremely flexible. Otherwise, coordinating childcare and household responsibilities becomes very difficult.

Working at home may be an option, though not an easy one. As Susan Strasser points out in *Never Done: A History of American Housework,* many of the work-at-home options that existed for women in the nineteenth century have been taken over by businesses and industries, or practically regulated out of existence: making clothing as a seamstress, taking in laundry, taking in boarders, and so on. Only the advent of home computers has started moving work back into the home. But a lot depends on the baby; a regular napper is not guaranteed. Most work-at-home mothers either work very odd hours, or find that they still need to hire childcare to get anything done. Babies (and children in general) create frequent and unpredictable interruptions. Once babies achieve mobility, around six months, they need to be chased around and watched closely. When my children are being quiet and letting me work without interruption, they are usually either asleep, or up to no good. Work without deadlines and with few phone calls, that can be divided up into very small, interruptable tasks,[19] is best for working at home with small children.

---

19 By what is known in computer science as the "Divide and Conquer" strategy; breaking a large problem up into smaller, solvable problems.

## *Making a budget*

Creating a household budget is something that many people never get around to doing. My husband says that it felt overwhelming to him at first, just trying to figure out where to start. But it will save you a lot of money in the long term if you sit down and figure out where your income should be going. Really there are only two steps to budgeting: make a plan, and then make sure that it happens.

It may be eye-opening to just track your spending for a week or two and see where your money is going. The little things can really add up.

To make a budget, the first thing you need to know is how much money is coming in each month. This is easy if you are paid monthly. If you are paid every other week, there are (on average) 2.25 pay periods per month (26 pay periods per 12 months). Or just figure two pay periods per month, and accept the two extra paychecks as a bonus. If you are paid weekly, there are 4.33 pay periods per month.

If your pay varies wildly, you can calculate an average pay over time, and then build a budget based on a somewhat lower amount (to give yourself more of a financial cushion to smooth out the bumps).

It's simplest to work with the net pay (after taxes and other payroll deductions), and base the budget on that. For expenses, such as car insurance, that you don't pay every month, the easiest way to budget for them is to figure out the annual cost, and divide to by twelve to get one month's cost.

Typical budget categories (and percentages of net household income) include[20]:

- Housing (25%)
- Utilities (5%)
- Transportation (10%)
- Food (5%)
- Personal money (5%)
- Clothing (2%)

---

20 Based in part on Dave Ramsey's quick budget tool at
**http://www.daveramsey.com/etc/budget_lite/**

- Household supplies (2%)
- Entertainment (5%)
- Medical/Health (5%)
- Giving (10%)
- Savings (5%)

If you have debts besides a mortgage or car loan to pay off, then you're going to have to reduce spending in some other categories to come up with the money.

If that budget sounds too dreary, Alexandra Stoddard listed a more liberal one in *Living Beautifully Together*. (Remember, though, that she wrote it from the perspective of an older woman, with an empty nest, living in a two-professional-incomes household.) This is how she put it:

- Necessities (70%)
- Decorating and art (6%)
- Nonessentials—little luxuries (5%)
- Gift giving, entertaining, and holidays (5%)
- Vacations and travel (7%)
- Savings (5%)
- Miscellaneous (2%)

It may not look like the most frugal budget, but actually it is highly frugal: cutting way back on the so-called necessities, in order to afford many of the so-called luxuries. The most important thing is to work out a plan that fits your life, and stick to it.

However you decide to allocate your money, you need to enforce the budget, one way or another. One way is to set aside cash for each category in envelopes; when the money is gone, it's gone. (Larger items, like mortgage or rent and car payments can be controlled by not signing up for more than you can afford.) Otherwise, you will have to track spending closely, with a ledger or a spreadsheet, to make sure that you're not overspending in any category. Whenever you do overspend, the money has to come from some other category.

Try especially to build up some savings before and during pregnancy. Right after the baby is born is a time when your budget is likely to be strained by unanticipated needs, and by breaks in routine, so build up a financial cushion beforehand to smooth out the bumps in spending.

## Reducing unbudgeted food expenditures

Many times when we are busy with chores or errands, we run out of food, at least of food that is convenient to grab and eat, and then, driven by crashing blood sugar levels, we grab some kind of fast food. This gets expensive, fast. Better to plan ahead, and have some emergency rations on hand. Then when we are hungry and busy and in need of immediate carbohydrates, it will be there. Maybe keep some emergency food at home, and some in the car. We don't do this all the time, ourselves, but it would definitely pay.

In general, making a weekly meal plan can save you some serious dollars over the course of the year.[21] It's hard to figure out what to make when you are hungry, which is why you often hear, "There's nothing to eat!" in a kitchen full of ingredients. And, of course, it's best to start cooking before you're starving, too.

With a baby coming, it would be wise to fill up the freezer with nutritious, cooked food. For the second baby, we made huge batches of beef stew, and froze them in meal-size containers. Pressure canning is another option, if you have the equipment.

Pregnant women often have cravings for some foods, and strong aversions to others. Pregnancy itself creates a need for about 300 more calories per day, which is only a few dollars more in the food budget. So while you might have to adjust the kinds of foods you buy, the budget amount need not change much.

---

21 Really, what most convenience products are offering is the convenience of not having to think about what you are doing. Using convenience foods or eating out doesn't really save you time, it just saves you some thinking and planning. This also holds true for nonfood convenience products, such as disposable diapers. It's amazing how much money people (I do not except myself) will pay, to avoid having to think. See the Family Rituals section near the end of the book for thoughts about how to use rituals to save on thinking and money at the same time.

## Sabbaths, days of rest, and feasts

The Bible, in God's instructions to the Jews about Sabbaths, tithes, feasts, seventh-year rests, and jubilee years, makes it clear that regular times of rest, refreshment, and celebration are very important. If God needed a day of rest after six days of work, maybe we do too. I could not have made it through graduate school to get my Ph.D without taking a Sabbath rest every Sunday. It actually saved me time, by helping me work more effectively the other six days of the week. I'm still trying to figure out how to have a really restful Sabbath with small children around. One good book about keeping the Sabbath is Marva Dawn's *Keeping the Sabbath Wholly*. She says there are four aspects of Sabbath observance: ceasing, resting, embracing, and feasting. (I don't want to mandate keeping the Sabbath, or any other Old Testament observance, but there does seem to be some value to voluntary observance, as a personal act of faith.)

I also budget a little of my personal money for a Sabbath treat every week. Usually five dollars or less, but this keeps me from feeling too deprived. In the middle of the week, when I'm busy being superfrugal, I always have Sunday to look forward to. One mistake that I've seen not-so-rich people make, is to cut way back on *everything*, always spending money on needs, but never on wants, until it gets to be too much, and then they go and spend a *lot* more money than they could afford. It would be better to budget a little in the first place for this, if only a dollar or two a week. (This is one point where I disagree with Dave Ramsey.)

Likewise, I am no advocate of spending every waking minute on "productive" work, even though it may look more frugal on the surface. We were not made to work like machines.

## Paying your bills

It is very important that you get your bill-paying system working well before the baby is born. The birth of a baby will almost completely disrupt your household routine. Getting things in shape ahead of time can save you a lot of late fees and headaches later on.

Not to be pedantic, but to specify the process so that we can examine it, this is the basic bill-paying workflow:

1. Receive bill: via paper mail, e-mail, or online account statement.

2. Pay bill: by cash, check, credit card, online payment, or auto-payment.

3. File for records: in paper files, computer files (please back these up!), credit card or bank statements, checkbook, and/or a spending log.

In whatever form you receive your bills and pay them, this is the basic process. The important thing is to make sure that no bills fall through the cracks. Breakdowns in the process are most likely to occur between the first two steps, between receipt of bill and payment of bill, so focus on that first. If you make a notebook or spreadsheet or calendar of when each bill should arrive and will be due and a place to check off when it was last paid—not to mention in what forms you receive billing and make payment—you can prevent many breakdowns, or at least minimize the damage of one. Most people keep track of these things only in their head.

Then, make the whole process one of your personal rituals: the mail comes, it goes to a particular place in your home for processing, and as needed you set aside time to go through bills and pay them. Or make an online bill-paying ritual at the computer. Whatever works for you.

## *Building up your savings*

Having a baby will stretch your budget out of shape, so you need to be building up some reserves. Putting cash away in a savings account, certificate of deposit, or money market account is one way to save; you receive low interest returns, but they have high liquidity so you can get at the money when you need it. Don't just save for baby expenses; save for emergency expenses as well.

Another way to save, if you have access to them through your employer or spouse's employer or some other way, is to save in a Flexible Spending Account (FSA) or Health Savings Account (HSA). You determine how much you want to save in the account, and your employer deducts the money from the paychecks and deposits it. The amount you can save in one is limited, but it is exempt from federal income tax as long as you spend it on health-related expenditures and follow the distribution rules. See IRS Publication 969[22] for the details of the different kinds of accounts, and for what are allowed as "qua-

---

22 IRS Publication 969 is online at **http://www.irs.gov/pub/irs-pdf/p969.pdf**

lified medical expenditures". One impact of the recent health care reform is that over-the-counter medications (except for insulin) are no longer reimbursable from these kinds of accounts, so if you want to use these funds for prenatal vitamins, you will need a prescription.

FSAs and HSAs differ. Flexible spending accounts are "use it or lose it": the year's savings can only be used for health-related expenses incurred in the calendar year. Since you have to decide how much to save at the beginning of the year, you have to make a calculated guess about when you are going to get pregnant. Guess wrong, and you could lose your money (or be forced to spend it on something else, to avoid losing it). HSA account balances roll over into the following years, and you can change how much you are saving in the middle of the year. But you need to have a high-deductible health plan (HDHP), and no other health coverage, to open a health savings account. Generally, high-deductible plans are best for people who are either very healthy or very ill, and who can afford to pay the high deductibles.

With HSAs, you also hold more responsibility for bookkeeping, and keeping track of receipts for health care expenditures. You file a tax form (Form 8889) with your federal income taxes to reconcile what you withdrew from the account with what you actually spent on health care (and pay taxes on any excess withdrawal). So this will complicate your tax preparation somewhat.

With an HSA, you can only withdraw money that is in the account. If you're just getting an account started, you may have to pay medical expenses with other savings, and then pay again into the HSA before you can reimburse yourself, which could be a strain on household cash flow. With FSAs, you may withdraw funds before you've contributed them to the account.

## *Investing*

"Don't invest money in things that you don't understand."—Old proverb

Staying at home with one income, there is usually not a lot of extra money to invest. The best investment to make is in expanding your frugal skills, and learning how to "live cheap but good" (title of an old frugality book[23]). In conventional investing, the deck is stacked against you in favor of people who have a lot more money than you do, and who know how to play the game a lot better than you do. Then, most of what you do earn will be taxable. So it's better to keep your money at home and improve the economic efficiency of your home first. Investing time and thought can pay off quite well.

There's a Biblical example of this in Proverbs, chapter 31: "She considers a field, and buys it, and with the fruit of her hands she plants a vineyard" (RSV). In those times, wine was a basic household necessity, because of the lack of clean water. This idealized woman planted a vineyard to be able to make wine for her household, and to be rid of the need to buy wine from others. (On the other hand, she couldn't afford to do this until she was older and her children were mostly grown, even after years of frugal living.)

So, I say that one of the best investments to start out with is to buy clothes drying racks or a clothesline (indoor, outdoor, or retractable), or perhaps some plastic clothes hangers for hanging things up in the bathroom. This gives you the freedom to avoid using the dryer. Using someone else's dryer is particularly expensive; it can cost a couple bucks at the laundromat to just half-dry a load of clothes. I figure that I am saving about $200 per year by hanging clothes to dry instead of using the apartment laundry, using less than $30 worth of racks and hangers. So the racks pay for themselves very quickly, and go on to give an annual return of several hundred percent—for a very low risk, and not much time and energy on my part. That's a return that you're almost guaranteed to never find in the stock market, and it is *tax free*. Now there is that much money that you can put into something else, or that your breadwinner does not have to work for anymore. The more you do this sort of thing, the more options you will have about how to live and how many babies you can afford. I call it microinvesting.

Some people find that hanging clothes to dry makes them too stiff and uncomfortable. Or ventilating the home to get rid of the excess moisture in the air lets out too much heat (or cooling). For them, it might be better to keep using the dryer and economize elsewhere. But hanging to dry does save a lot of wear on clothes (from the agitation of the dryer).

---

23 *How to Live Cheap but Good*, by Martin Poriss, who insisted that one spoon, one knife, and one pot was enough to start cooking and eating with.

See *The Complete Tightwad Gazette* (which is another good investment, whether you buy it new or used, or just borrow it from the library) by Amy Dacyczyn for more about how to calculate your "hourly wage" for economizing at home. Hanging up laundry to dry takes me about 20 minutes, to hang up three loads. This saves me $3.75 (at least) for not having to use the apartment building's coin laundry. If I did an hour's worth of it, that would be $3.75 times 3. So my hourly wage for it is $11.25, with no income tax. Also, it probably saves me a little on the putting-away time because I can gather items that go together off the racks at the same time.

Another good investment around the house is a slow cooker (such as a CrockPot®). It is one of the most underutilized money-saving gadgets around. You might have one of these already. New ones cost about $30 and up, used ones maybe $5-$10. If you replace one takeout meal per week with a slow cooker meal, you could easily save five dollars a week—over two hundred dollars a year—again, tax free. It requires only a few pennies worth of electricity to run on High all day. Cooking a simple recipe like a roast only requires a few basic ingredients, and very little preparation time. Clean-up is easy if you fill it with hot water and a little dish soap after the meal, and let it soak for a bit. The slow cooker could pay for itself in six to eight weeks; 400% profit after a year.

Saving money by shopping for sales and using coupons is fine, but remember that they are essentially bait to get you into the store and spending money. Stick to buying the things that you need and will use, and will get good value from.

Finally, one thing that saves us a great deal of money is a weekly meal plan. When the grocery store ads arrive, I quickly skim over them and make a short list of good sale items to buy. Amy Dacyczyn recommends keeping a price book to be able to recognize good prices. After shopping, I write out a quick meal plan based on what we actually bought. Nothing fancy, sometimes just: "Pasta" or "Rice". I often refine it and build on it as the week goes on, I find ingredients that I can use up in the meals, and flashes of inspiration come to me. This helps me waste less food, and at the same time make more nutritious meals. I plan easier meals for the days that I know will be busier.

Once you've optimized your household processes as much as you can, the next thing to invest in is things that will bring in a little money. See *The Incredible Secret Money Machine* by Don Lancaster for hints on how to get started. The basic idea is that you start a little side business, with only a very small amount of start-up money. Then, you invest a large amount of time into developing and selling a good product, and use the money that you earn this way to build up the business. He recommends having a number of small businesses going, to diversify your sources of income, but I would say that a stay-at-home parent can probably manage only one or two or three at a time. At least when young children are involved.

The reason that this works so well for Mr. Don is that he only creates money machines that bring in a *200% return* on cash flow. That means, for every one dollar he puts into it, he gets at least three dollars back. He only creates money machines where he really enjoys the work, and doesn't mind investing a lot of his time and sweat. And then he works hard to make sure that he is taking advantage of every tax break that he can, to keep the money for himself or to plow back into the money machine. Most businesses have *much* leaner profit margins than that. Mr. Don also keeps his overhead very low—no employees, no equipment that doesn't pay for itself within two months, no fancy office.

After you have some money machines going, the next thing to invest in is things that are just plain good—small-scale philanthropy. Ecclesiastes 11:1: "Cast your bread upon the waters, for you will find it after many days" (RSV). Thieves steal, moths eat, rust corrodes, banks close, governments tax, but investments in good works will stand. For Christians, I suggest investing in ministries that work to alleviate both spiritual and material poverty.

## Life insurance

This would also be a good time to think about getting life insurance. The odds of either parent dying before the baby grows up is small, but it is not zero. Also, since insurance companies often base premiums on Body Mass Index (calculated based on your height and weight), age, and general state of health, getting life insurance before you start gaining pregnancy weight may save you some money. However, you should find out how often the premiums reset—as you get older and in worse health, your premiums can greatly increase. If you remain in good health, the company is likely to offer you opportunities to purchase additional coverage from them.

There are two main kinds of life insurance, whole life and term. Term life insurance is generally recommended for younger people, who are starting families and taking on mortgages. It is renewable for a specified term, often 20 or 30 years, or up to a specified age. At the end of the term, you have to sign up for a new, much more costly policy if you want to stay insured.

Whole life insurance is sold as insurance with an investment component. The advantage of whole life is that you can keep renewing it as long as you live, although the premiums may increase at times. There are also savings that accumulate, which you may be able to cash out or borrow against, but this depends on the policy.

The most sensible advice I've seen for deciding on whole life versus term life insurance is to take out term life insurance for the years where you are raising a family, paying for a house, and sending children to college, and to also take out a smaller whole-life policy, if you want to maintain coverage after the term insurance runs out (at which point your life insurance needs should be very much less).

There are varying schools of thought on how much life insurance to take out for each parent. Some people want to cover funeral expenses, and children's college expenses, and allow the surviving parent to take an extended time off work, and also be able to pay off the whole mortgage, if one parent dies. Others want to mainly cover funeral expenses and the transition to a life without the deceased parent. It's important to realize that Social Security provides some life insurance coverage for most people. Each child under eighteen is eligible for benefits if a parent dies, and the surviving spouse is also eligible for benefits, if caring for children under age sixteen (and will also receive retirement benefits at retirement age). The total amount of benefits per family is limited, but it can substantially reduce the amount of life insurance that you need to purchase. Workers age 25 and over receive a Social Security Statement each year, with estimates of the monthly benefits that their survivors could receive. Likewise, Social Security provides some disability benefits, although it can be difficult to prove that you are sufficiently disabled.

The general consensus is that stay-at-home parents should also be covered by life insurance, because all the work that they do at home is expensive to replace by paid labor.

You should also consider the effects of inflation if you purchase life insurance; the value of the coverage erodes over time as prices rise. Many prices for goods and services have doubled over the last twenty years.

Life insurance for children is yet another question. On the plus side, it may be renewable after childhood, regardless of health status, so it can be valuable for children who become sick with chronic diseases, for whom regular life insurance would be prohibitively expensive. On the other hand, few children die in childhood these days, so the premiums can be a total waste of money. I would recommend taking out a smaller policy on your children, if you get life insurance for them at all.

In any case, don't commit to any insurance policy until you understand it thoroughly —premiums add up considerably over time. Insurance agents work on commission, so make sure they sell you only what you really want.

While you're planning for your eventual demise, you might consider who would make a good guardian for your children, in the unlikely event that both parents die in an untimely manner. This is best specified in a will, but professional estate planning assistance is expensive. There are books and software that can help you declare your wishes.

## *Tax implications of having a child*

Having a child will probably have a significant impact on the amount of state and federal income tax that you will have to pay. The IRS has a withholding calculator[24] to help you figure out how much a baby will affect your taxes.

For tax purposes, the baby counts as a dependent. This reduces your taxable income, Also, there is a child tax credit of $1000[25]—credited to your tax due. If your household income is low, having a baby may qualify you for the Earned Income Tax Credit. There is also a Child Care Tax Credit, if you use childcare to care for the child while you work.[26]

---

24 The IRS withholding calculator can be found at
**http://www.irs.gov/individuals/index.html**
25 Assuming (December 2010) that Congress renews the Bush tax cuts, as seems likely.
26 Both parents have to earn income, and the childcare provider can't be one of your other children, or a relative. If you hire a nanny or babysitter to provide care in your home, you become an employer and will probably have to pay Social Security, Medicare, and unemployment taxes for

Altogether, having a child (or two or three) can substantially reduce your taxes. There is also a tax credit for adoption.[27] The IRS has a web page of topics that affect parents.[28] Watch for income limits on tax breaks (though most of these are set very high).

If one parent quits work to take care of the baby, the decrease in income may put you in a lower tax bracket. But if the household income is on the higher side, above $70,000 or so per year, the alternative minimum tax (AMT) may come into play—this is where consulting a tax professional can be helpful. Also see the IRS's "Alternative Minimum Tax Assistant for Individuals" calculator.[29] (Congress has been stalling on fixing the AMT for years, and keeps patching up only the deductible limits, so you will need up-to-date advice.) The big issues with the AMT are that it disallows various deductions and tax credits, and that it has not been indexed for inflation, so more and more solidly middle-class families are being affected by it.

If you're sure that the baby is going to be born before the end of the year, it is possible to run the withholding calculator and adjust your tax withheld (by filing a new W4 form —you can do this at any time) early in the year. The baby doesn't need to be born first; tax should be withheld based on your expected tax bill. The only problem with that is that the pregnancy might end in a miscarriage or stillbirth.[30] Only babies that are alive

---

them—see IRS Publication 926, "Household Employer's Tax Guide" (available at **http://www.irs.gov/publications/p926/index.html**) and IRS Publication 503, "Child and Dependent Care Expenses" (available at **http://www.irs.gov/pub/irs-pdf/p503.pdf**). Maximum credit for one child seems to be $3000; $6000 for multiple children.

27 The health care reform, in the Patient Protection and Affordable Care Act of 2010, Section 10909, increased the adoption tax credit to a maximum of $13,170, made it retroactive to January 1, 2010, made it a refundable credit (so it can go toward a tax refund), and renewed it through 2011.

28 **http://www.irs.gov/individuals/parents/index.html**

29 The "Alternative Minimum Tax Assistant for Individuals" can be found at **http://www.irs.gov/businesses/small/article/0,,id=150703,00.html**

30 The risk of miscarriage is not low in the early months of pregnancy, so you may want to wait until the second trimester to adjust withholding. The risk of stillbirth is smaller, about 1 in 160, according to the American College of Obstetricians and Gynecologists: **http://www.acog.org/from_home/publications/press_releases/nr02-20-09-2.cfm** On the other hand, the odds of having twins are about 1 in 35, according to Denise and Alan Fields,

when they are born, and are listed as live births on their birth certificates, count for the dependent exemption. I also wouldn't do this if the baby was due in late December—if the baby waits until the new year to be born, you won't be able to claim the baby, and will owe tax (and possibly penalties as well).

If you wait until the baby is born to adjust your withholding, that should increase your take-home pay, and improve your cash flow for the first months of the baby's life. But remember to reevaluate your withholding at the beginning of the next year.

## *Help from the government?*

There are a lot of government aid programs around to help lower-income families with children. Living on a single income makes you likely to qualify for some level of help. (Whether or not you should avail yourself of this aid is another question; see the end of this section.) The various programs each have different income and asset limits. Generally, the implementations of the programs vary by state, as the states have most of the responsibility for administering them. Here are some of the larger programs:

- ◆ Temporary Assistance to Needy Families (TANF)—help for very needy families to achieve economic self-sufficiency.

- ◆ WIC—nutrition and health care referral program for pregnant, postpartum and breastfeeding women, and children under the age of five. In 2008, an average of 8.7 million people received WIC benefits.[31] WIC encourages breast-feeding (including providing peer counseling) , but provides formula for mothers who do not breastfeed.

- ◆ Food stamps—assistance for purchasing groceries. Thirty-five million Americans were receiving food stamps in June 2009.[32]

- ◆ Medicaid—assistance with health care costs for some low-income people.

in *Baby Bargains.*

31 According to the USDA's WIC Fact Sheet at **http://www.fns.usda.gov/wic/WIC-Fact-Sheet.pdf**

32 As reported by Reuters, 9/3/2009:
**http://www.reuters.com/article/domesticNews/idUSTRE58250T20090903**

- CHIP—Children's Health Insurance Program, health insurance coverage for children and pregnant women who do not quite qualify for Medicaid. It has recently been expanded to cover 11 million children.[33]

You might want to take a look to see what you qualify for. Where to start? Start with your state government's web site, or with a social worker. Or complete the questionnaire at GovBenefits.gov.[34] It is long, and asks too many personal questions (in my opinion), but it may be helpful. I filled it out with some mildly untrue data, and came up with a couple of dozen programs that my fictitious persona might qualify for.

But even if you qualify for assistance, it doesn't mean that you have to accept it. Government programs come with all the hassles of government bureaucracy—endless and intrusive paperwork, waiting periods or waiting lists, inconsistent application of rules and procedures, bureaucrats on personal power trips, and sometimes requirements to appear in person. Also, government programs may have limited funding, and can run out of money before they get to you. Record numbers of Americans are receiving assistance of one kind or another, and some government agencies are simply overwhelmed. You might want to estimate your hourly wage before you start applying for aid.

Also, consider the effect of accepting aid on you—will it dull your self-reliance and your initiative to develop your own resources? My husband and I have accepted the responsibility of providing for our children ourselves. For this reason, I refuse to apply for government aid until my family really needs it. I would feel guilty to take aid that I didn't need. We are not at our last rope; there are many frugal strategies that I could dust off and use if money got too tight for us. For me, taking all the tax advantages that I can is one thing, and lining up for a handout is another.

But if you are truly in need, don't feel guilty about applying for benefits, and drawing on other social resources. You've been paying for this safety net with your taxes for years. Poor people often have a great deal of experience in navigating the assistance mazes and hurdles; middle class people who find themselves in need of help are at a disadvantage. My advice is to apply quickly once you find yourself in need, because it often takes weeks for any real assistance to actually reach you. Be persistent, because some-

---

33 According to the program overview at

**http://www.cms.hhs.gov/LowCostHealthInsFamChild/**

34 The questionnaire is available at **http://www.govbenefits.gov/govbenefits_en.portal**

times a lot of obstacles are placed in the way of applicants, to save programs money by weeding out all but the very desperate. Work hard to get off assistance as quickly as you can.

## *Spiritual Health*

Spiritual health is, perhaps surprisingly to some, an important aspect of frugality. This is because spiritual problems are frequently at the root of overspending. Feelings of inferiority, insecurity, discontent, ingratitude, and guilt can lead to overspending in an attempt to compensate for the perceived lack. So stop and take a look once in a while at what you're buying and why you are buying it.

Sooner or later, everyone needs to find a lasting source of spiritual satisfaction; the high from a new purchase is fleeting, and will not last long. Most shopaholics are not happy people at heart. Even having a baby is not as spiritually fulfilling as you might think. All that I'm going to say about Jesus here is that I've found something with him that I have never found anywhere else.

Spiritual growth requires some solitude to get started. It's not that it never happens in the context of community, but it does need solitude to truly flourish. By solitude, I mean a regular time to be still and face the truth. This time is very difficult to get when you have a baby or young children, so get as much as you can before you start having babies. It is a good investment.

Another reason to pay particular attention to spiritual needs before and during pregnancy is that having a baby is a major life event, and lots of buried issues from your past tend to bubble up and resurface. In pregnancy, dreams become much more vivid and disturbing—one way that these issues make themselves known.

Jim and Sally Conway, in *Women in Midlife Crisis*,[35] recommend taking these four steps in the growth process (they are talking about choosing to grow spiritually in the midst of a midlife crisis, but their advice is equally applicable to dealing with becoming a parent):

    1.   Spend time reflecting—alone.

---

35 Page 361.

2.  Meet with a group of people with whom you can talk.

3.  Get ideas from outside sources—reading and learning.

4.  Allow God to be involved.

I have a few more suggestions:

- Make peace with the past. Getting counseling can be a good investment.

- Look for some mentors in parenthood—older parents who have successfully and joyfully raised children.

- Consider going away for a spiritual retreat, alone or as a couple. Check your local classified ads, or try some online retreat directories, to find a place to go. Or stay home, or at a motel, or go to the park, or to a library...the point is to step out of your normal routine for a time.

- If you pray, you can pray for yourselves as parents, for the pregnancy, and for the growing child.

# 2

# During Pregnancy

The good thing about pregnancy is that it gives you a few months to get ready for the baby's arrival.

## *Finding out*

If you are charting your cycles of fertility, the first sign of pregnancy you will see is that the temperature does not dip for the beginning of menstruation. It just stays high, and there is no period, or there is only a small amount of bleeding.

Pregnancy is usually detectable by conventional, cheap pregnancy tests by twelve to fourteen days after ovulation—typically right around the start of the first missed period. (If you don't know when you ovulated, figure at least 19 days after sex.[36]) Follow the test directions, a positive result that only shows up after the test's time limit is probably not a true positive. I can attest, though, that conventional, cheap pregnancy tests sometimes give false negative readings: I was seven weeks pregnant with my daughter before I learned that I was pregnant, after two "negative" pregnancy tests earlier on.

One downside of early testing is that more of the pregnancies that end in very early miscarriages are discovered. Not all "late periods" are really periods.

If you can't afford even a cheap pregnancy test, but still want to test, then check the yellow pages for a local crisis pregnancy center, which may offer free pregnancy tests and

---

36 According to peeonastick.com: **http://www.peeonastick.com/hptfaq.html**

counseling on how to afford to have and keep your baby, including information about and referrals to local resources.

A blood sample for a lab pregnancy test can also be drawn at the doctor's or midwife's office.

# *Deciding when to leave work*

Here are some factors to consider about when you should leave work to begin a maternity leave (or quit outright):

- ◆ What maternity benefits does the job have? Does it offer paid leave or unpaid leave? Is the company too small to have to abide by the Family and Medical Leave Act? (Many small companies offer comparable leave, though not required by law.)

- ◆ How much time and energy will be needed to prepare the household for a new baby?

- ◆ Does the job involve exposure to chemicals that might be dangerous to a developing baby?

- ◆ Does the job involve traveling by air? Airlines vary in how far along you can be in pregnancy before they won't allow you to fly.

- ◆ Is the work too heavy, dangerous, or stressful for a pregnant woman?

- ◆ Is the workload simply too great?

- ◆ Is there an emerging health issue with this pregnancy?

- ◆ Are there ergonomic issues? Pregnant women need more frequent bathroom breaks, and have difficulty reaching as far or standing as long.[37]

- ◆ What health benefits are affected by the timing of your leave? Will you lose health care coverage if you quit?

- ◆ What is your body telling you? Pregnancy is hard work for your body, and will tax your physical resources heavily even if you're not working.

---

[37] *Extraordinary Ergonomics*, listed in the Print Resources section, is one book that highlights some of the workplace ergonomic issues raised by pregnancy.

◆ Is the household financial situation ready for a drop in income, if the leave is not at full pay?

Of working women who intend to return to work, most work well into the third trimester, although slogging through the fatigue of the first and third trimesters is difficult.

## *Childbirth choices and preparation*

The choice of who to go to for prenatal care matters more than you might think, because this is the person who will likely be caring for you and the baby during labor and childbirth. It's true that you can change providers whenever you want, even during labor. But the longer you wait, the harder it can be to find someone willing to take you on. You have some time to decide—many obstetricians don't want to see pregnant women until they are three months pregnant.

It is important to educate yourself about childbirth; practices and customs have changed greatly since your mother gave birth—mostly for the better, but not entirely. Maternity and newborn services are major sources of revenue for hospitals, so there is a lot of competition for patients. And a lot of room for you to save money and be frugal, if you want to be. Not to mention saving yourself a lot of trouble.

The first thing you need to know is that technology comes with a price tag. Fancy machines cost a lot of money, and hospitals want them to earn their keep.

Second, those fancy, shiny machines do surprisingly little to make childbirth safer for the mother and baby. In fact, they sometimes make it less safe. A low-risk pregnancy is probably better off without them—even many doctors say so. Innovations like ultrasounds and continuous fetal monitoring in labor, which were once reserved for high-risk cases, are now routinely used on practically all pregnant and laboring women, with little consideration about whether their benefits outweigh the risks. Our perceptions of risk and safety have also changed greatly in the past few decades—yet another example of what I call "safety inflation". Actually, the main purposes for technology in the hospital are to reduce staffing costs (humans are even more expensive than machines), and to prevent expensive litigation.

The same thing goes for other interventions in the childbirth process. Inductions are common, but they are often much more painful for the mother, and they frequently fail. A caesarean section is quick and convenient for the doctor,[38] but painful, difficult to recover from, and expensive for the mother, running roughly twice the cost for a vaginal birth.[39] Most of them are not even necessary: Consumer Reports Health lists c-sections as one of the most over-used medical procedures in the U.S.[40] The caesarean rate in the U.S. was 31.8% in 2007,[41] and is still rising. Not frugal! I have nothing against medical care that is medically necessary, but I have to question the utility of a supposedly life-saving procedure that, in my estimation, is one of the top factors driving down the birth rate in the United States.[42]

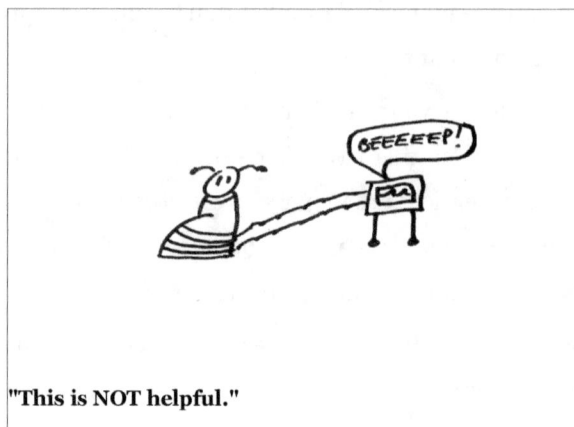

"This is NOT helpful."

Not only is technology expensive, but personalized care is expensive, too. The typical prenatal visit with an OB is only fifteen minutes, which is ridiculously short. (I have

---

38 Like some maintenance guys that my husband once worked with, doctors and hospitals can be a little too casual about breaking things—because they think that they can fix whatever they break.

39 Attempted vaginal births that end in c-sections can cost more than a scheduled c-section.

40 See their online article at **http://www.consumerreports.org/health/free-highlights/manage-your-health/needless_surgeries.htm**

41 See the National Vital Statistics System report "Births: Preliminary Data for 2007", online at **http://www.cdc.gov/nchs/data/nvsr/nvsr57/nvsr57_12.pdf**

42 Some others are: car seat laws, college tuition costs, and rising taxes. Safety and a higher standard of living come at a price.

one-hour appointments with my midwives.) Most labor care will be done by nurses you haven't met before. Most labor monitoring will be done by machine. Yet the attitude of the people attending and supporting the labor can significantly affect the progress and experience of labor and birth.

Some of us are two or more generations away from the last homebirths (or even natural childbirths) in our families. The knowledge of what a natural birth is really like has been practically lost, for many people.[43] The horrors of inhumanely managed birth in the hospital are often confused with the natural pains and labor of a normal childbirth "in the wild". Hospital birth can actually be a lot more painful than homebirth, because there is so much more that the mother has to cope with in the hospital: strange environment, unfamiliar people, monitors, exams, mysterious medical equipment, procedures, interruptions, distractions, arbitrary rules.

Sadly, many doctors and nurses still vilify the simple observations of Dr. Grantly Dick-Read and Dr. Robert Bradley. (Sometimes I just have to wonder what doctors are being taught in those medical schools. ) Dick-Read observed in the Twenties that fear in childbirth can lead to tension, and tension can greatly increase pain and difficulty in labor.[44] Bradley observed in the Forties that women, like other mammals, birth most easily in a dark, quiet, calm place, with interference kept to a minimum.[45] Both were forerunners of the modern natural childbirth movement. Many people have observed that the standard reclining position for giving birth in the hospital is actually one of the hardest positions to give birth from, though convenient for the doctors and nurses.

## What a natural childbirth looks like

Labor starts in the baby's good time. Both mother and baby work together for the baby to be born: the baby has to rotate into a good position for birth, and the mother's walking, rocking, and swaying helps the baby to move. Later in the birth process, the baby has to twist and turn to navigate through the birth canal.

---

43 *Adventures in Natural Childbirth*, listed in the Print Resources section, is a book of natural childbirth birth stories.

44 His book *Childbirth Without Fear*, first published in 1933, is still well worth reading.

45 Likewise, Dr. Bradley's book *Husband-Coached Childbirth* is also well worth reading.

Labor is as much mental work as physical work for the mother.[46] She enters an an altered mental state as early labor turns into active labor, and moans and breathes to ride out the contractions. There is little talking, as verbal processing is not compatible with the "labor trance".

Transition is the hardest stage of labor, and it is usually the part where the mother feels like she's not going to make it through. But it is short, and the difficulty of labor levels off.

In the pushing stage, the mother's instincts tell her what position to birth in. After a while, the "fetal ejection reflex" takes over, and it becomes very difficult not to push. The mother instinctively pants to slow down the pushes if the baby is descending too quickly, to allow time for her tissues to stretch, and minimize tearing.

Then the baby is born, and scooped up to rest on the mother's soft tummy. The first bath can wait—vernix protects the baby's skin. Many babies will breastfeed for a little while right after birth. This is the time for the mother and baby to meet each other and begin the bonding process. A hormonal rush of oxytocin, the bonding hormone, is re-leased, which helps the placenta to detach and be expelled, and the uterus to shrink down and stop bleeding.

The mother and baby spend a few days in bed together, bonding and getting a good start to breastfeeding.

This may seem like an overly romanticized view of childbirth, but actually it's not nearly as idealized as you might think. I have seen it for myself in my two homebirths. I can't guarantee that every woman can birth babies as easily as I can, but it's clear that many could. About 15% of women homebirthing with a midwife end up at the hospital, for one reason or another, but the other 85% do all right at home.[47]

There is a complex interplay of hormones and instincts in the birth process. Modern managed births, steeped in the languages of rationality, science, and efficiency, tend to disrupt the natural process at every step, leading to greater pain and greater danger for

46 Some commentators claim that the "labor/travail/pain" in Genesis Chapter 3 Verse 16 is the same Hebrew word as "toil" in verse 17 (Adam's curse). I have not tried to read the Hebrew myself, but it sounds plausible. Personally, I think that the toil of childbearing is not limited to childbirth, but also includes the exhausting level of care that all small children require.

47 These are numbers that I read a long time ago; naturally they vary from midwife to midwife.

both mother and baby, who may then need to be rescued with medical care. Birthing is primarily an intuitive and instinctual process, and one that cannot be entirely controlled.

## Benefits of natural childbirth

The benefits of natural childbirth are numerous. First, it allows the body's natural pain relief system to go to work: endorphins are released, leading to a "birth high" (that can be "better than LSD", according to some). The painful part of a normal natural labor and birth lasts only for a few hours, and ends when the baby is born. What pain there is comes in waves, with rests in between—it is not constant. Finally, labor pain is a "good pain", not a pain of injury—it comes from the body doing its work to stretch and push out the baby. Drugs are not the only form of pain relief available; being free to change position, soaking in warm water, getting some massage or counterpressure, and being free of distractions that disrupt inward focus can all reduce the pain of childbirth, or increase the ability to cope with it.

In the pushing stage, an unmedicated mother has an easier time of pushing: being able to feel the descent of the baby, being able to change positions if needed, being able to ease off if her body needs a few more moments to stretch. This means fewer instrumental deliveries and birth injuries, which is good for both mother and baby.

With natural childbirth, there is less for the body to recover from afterward, with no lingering drug aftereffects. This applies to the baby as well as to the mother: naturally born babies are more alert after birth, and get a better start to breastfeeding.

## Childbirth and prenatal care providers

Check again what hospitals and clinics and providers are covered under your insurance. Here are the different options for health care providers and other helpers for prenatal and maternity care:

- ◆ **Obstetricians (OBs):** Most women choose these for prenatal care and to attend the birth. They are qualified to do caesarean surgeries.

- **Family Practice/General Practice Doctors:** Many of these are now barred by their malpractice insurance, or what-have-you, from attending births. The ones that do attend births are usually the ones that like to attend births.

- **Nurse-Midwives:** Nurses with additional training in midwifery. Certified nurse-midwives (CNMs) typically work in hospitals and clinics, under physician supervision, but some can be found in birth centers, and a few even attend home births. Their professional organization is the American College of Nurse-Midwives.[48]

- **Midwives:** Midwives have specialized midwifery training. Some are Certified Midwives, who work primarily in hospitals. Direct entry midwives (DEMs), or certified professional midwives (CPMs; if they have qualified for certification) primarily attend home births (though not all states allow this). Homebirth midwives very rarely have malpractice insurance, because it is very rarely available to them. Some of them are members of MANA (Midwives Alliance of North America).[49] If insurance covers the services of homebirth midwives at all, it will probably be as out-of-network providers.

- **Traditional Midwives:** These midwives have trained in their communities by apprenticeship, rather than by formal education, generally.

- **Nurses:** Nurses provide most of the hands-on maternity care in hospitals. One disadvantage of hospital birth is that you probably won't meet the nurses who will care for you until you show up in labor. (It is possible to request a different nurse, if you don't like the one you were assigned, by speaking to the charge nurse on duty.)

- **Doulas:** The doula's job is to take care of the mother. Some doulas specialize in helping during childbirth, some specialize in postpartum care (such as cleaning, helping with meals and childcare, and breastfeeding mentorship), and some do all of the above. You can find doulas through DONA International (formerly known as Doulas of North America),[50] or from keeping your eye out

---

48 http://www.midwife.org/

49 http://mana.org/

50 http://www.dona.org/

for local advertisements. Typically, doula fees run several hundred dollars, or $25 per hour and up, but they are well worth it. Some doulas claim that their fees are reimbursable through health savings accounts, but I'm not sure if the IRS agrees.

- ◆ **Childbirth educators:** Teachers of childbirth education classes, teaching either through an institution, or independently. Some teach from specific childbirth philosophies, such as Lamaze or the Bradley method.

- ◆ **Friends and Family:** This is one of the times when you will need to draw on your social network.

## *The politics and economics of maternity care*

There are many factors that will affect the maternity care you receive.[51] These are some of the forces at play:

- ◆ Malpractice insurance is becoming more and more expensive, which forces some obstetricians out of practice, and increases the workload of the rest.

- ◆ Decreased reimbursement from government aid programs (such as Medicaid), and from insurance companies, is another pressure on obstetricians to increase their patient throughput.

- ◆ Physicians (and hospitals) who are worried about being sued for malpractice take a more defensive approach to maternity care.

- ◆ Busy doctors who attend thirty or more births per month can't spend much time at any one birth (or on any one patient's prenatal care). Scheduled caesareans are fast and easy for them. In a group practice, you may get whoever is on call, rather than your own doctor, when you give birth.

- ◆ Doctors and midwives have an ongoing turf war over patients/clients. Not to mention their philosophical differences in how to care for them. (Certified

---

51 The article "Effects of Hospital Economics on Maternity Care" by Susan Hodges and Henci Goer (online at **http://www.yourbody-yourbirth.com/uploads/maternitycareandhospitaleconomics.pdf**) is an eye-opening look at the economic incentives for doctors and hospitals.

nurse-midwives are kind of in the middle, as are many individual doctors and midwives. But even the ones in the middle are facing a lot of pressure to practice more "efficiently".)

◆ Nurses (and nurse-midwives) are constrained by their hospitals' guidelines and culture, and by the preferences of the doctors that they work with.

◆ Doctors and nurses may have never been trained in how to support natural childbirth. Other skills, such as safely delivering breech babies vaginally, are disappearing at an alarming rate, as the older doctors with these skills retire, and the younger doctors have been trained to perform caesareans instead.

◆ Maternity and newborn care are a major part of most hospitals' revenue streams, and hospitals compete with each other for pregnant women.

◆ Hospitals try to increase their patient throughput to maximize revenue. In some hospitals, the standing policy is to give pitocin to all laboring women, to speed up their labors. (The greatly increased labor pains can be covered up with anesthesia.)

◆ The fancy machines at the hospital need to earn their keep. So do anesthesiologists.

◆ Doctors and hospitals sometimes have an economic incentive to label women as "high-risk", and to send babies to the NICU (neonatal intensive care unit).

◆ One way hospitals contain their costs is by not overstaffing—so expect that your nurse will have at least one other laboring woman to look after.

◆ Labors that are more actively managed are more predictable, for staffing purposes.

◆ Midwives in states where they are regulated need to practice within the limits of their license.

◆ Midwives attending homebirths in states where this is illegal or alegal need to keep a low profile, and may either be reluctant to transfer clients to the hospital, or may be overcautious, and transfer prematurely.

◆   Midwives practicing independently of a physician may need to resort to creative billing practices to receive reimbursement from insurance companies. Some insurance companies are now specifically excluding homebirths.

◆   Doulas who act as strong advocates for their hospital birth clients risk being banned (either personally or collectively) from the hospital.

◆   This country does not have a good system for transferring from a homebirth or unassisted birth to the hospital. Show up at the hospital without any documented prenatal care, and they will likely assume that you are a druggie and/or a mental case. (But you will still be treated; EMTALA, the Emergency Medical Treatment and Active Labor Act, applies to most hospitals.)

◆   Government-sponsored health care programs need to control costs. Midwives are cheaper than doctors (as can be seen in the British National Health Service), if you can keep them from spending too much time on any one patient.

◆   Childbirth educators connected with a hospital are often under pressure to teach parents what the hospital's "program" for childbirth is, and how to comply with it.

◆   Childbirth educators who teach independently often teach from a childbirth philosophy that the hospitals are not enthusiastic about supporting.

◆   Insurance companies are looking out for their bottom line. C-sections are expensive, but not as expensive as a long labor for an attempted vaginal birth that ends in a c-section. They seem to be starting to catch on that midwives can be cheaper than doctors, and just as safe, in a hospital or birth center setting.

◆   Most of the interested parties prefer to minimize deaths rather than morbidity (a catch-all term for other undesirable events, such as *almost* dying). The medical people are trying to minimize mortality rates. Parents don't want to lose a child (or a mother). Insurance companies know that they won't be receiving premiums for anyone that dies.

In short, everyone is looking out for their own interests, and you need to look out for yours. Failing to do so can end up causing you thousands of dollars extra, and lead to lasting scars, both physical and emotional. The physical scars from a caesarean can lead to complications in later pregnancies: higher rates of miscarriage, placenta previa, excessive bleeding, repeat c-section. Emotional scars can manifest themselves in postpartum depression or Post Traumatic Stress Syndrome. Even just being labelled on your medical records as a "gestational diabetic" or "failure to progress" case can lead to adverse effects later on—by constraining your options in later pregnancies, and by creating feelings of being physically inadequate to give birth. About a third of U.S. hospitals now have official VBAC (vaginal birth after caesarean) bans, and many more have *de facto* VBAC bans.[52] (It is worth asking how these hospitals plan to handle other obstetric emergencies that require immediate c-sections, if they can't handle VBAC uterine rupture cases.)

The simplest way to have fewer things happen to you at the hospital is to not be there for as long. Consider waiting until you are definitely in active labor (labor that is too active for you to do much besides labor, water broken, etc.) to leave for the hospital. If you aren't showing some signs of active labor when you get there, they will probably send you back home anyway.

For myself I prefer natural childbirth at home with a midwife, because I do not need or want more medicalized care. It is the option that balances safety and cost for me. It costs more out of pocket, but I get a lot more personal care, and it gives me the best chance for having uncomplicated pregnancies in the future. Homebirth is a lot safer than most people think, if only because midwives are not allowed to perform the riskier procedures that are done in hospitals without a second thought.[53]

---

52 ICAN (International Cesarean Awareness Network) has created a database of hospitals with official or *de facto* VBAC bans (as determined by phone calls by ICAN members) at **http://www.ican-online.org/vbac-ban-info**

53 Midwives have incentives, therefore, to learn tricks such as Optimal Fetal Positioning (techniques encouraging the baby to get into a good position for labor; one of which is for the mother to avoid reclining positions in late pregnancy, and stay upright or leaning forward). There's also midwife Ina May Gaskin's "Sphincter Law": you can encourage the cervix (a sphincter muscle) to open by relaxing the muscles around the mouth and jaw (another set of sphincter muscles).

Ultimately, though, what I advocate for is autonomous birth,[54] and being able to make informed choices. No one is more concerned about the well-being of your baby (and mother and the rest of the family) than you are. For true informed consent, you need both reliable information, and real choices. It is all too easy for health care providers to manipulate decision-making, by selective delivery of information.

Remember, too, that the birth is for the baby. There is evidence that babies remember a lot more about how they were born than we give them credit for. Some of the old twin studies tried to differentiate between nature and nurture, by studying twins that were separated at birth and raised in different families. Researcher Thomas Bouchard noticed that some pairs of separated twins led surprisingly similar lives. One pair's first wives had the same name, and so did their second wives. The conclusion for some was that the twins' shared genes were responsible for these remarkable similarities. But this kind of reasoning has a serious flaw: it ignores the shared prenatal life that the twins led in the uterus before they were born. Maybe that shared life shaped their later choices as much as their shared genes did. And possibly the birth process is remembered as well.

I see that I haven't said anything about birth centers yet. Birth centers vary greatly. Some birth centers are connected with a hospital maternity unit, and can easily transfer clients over in an emergency. Some birth centers don't have any more emergency equipment or expertise than what a homebirth midwife would bring to your house. Probably most fall in between. Go and take a tour for yourself, and ask who works there: doctors, nurse-midwives, or regular midwives. Their licensing sets the limits of what they can do.

Finally, if you want to keep the placenta after the birth for any reason, you will probably be far better off with a midwife. Very few hospitals will put the placenta in the refrigerator so you can take it home (or let you put it in your own cooler). There are various reasons for wanting to keep the placenta: lotus birth (keeping the umbilical cord and placenta intact until they naturally separate from the baby), burying it and planting a tree over it as part of a birth ritual, or just eating it: fried; dried, ground, and encapsulated; raw; or incorporated into a smoothie.[55]

---

54 A term coined (as far as I know), by Linda Hessel, and I hope that she someday gets around to finishing her book on the subject.

## *Starting prenatal care*

Once you have chosen which type of health care provider you want for your maternity care, go interview a few, and make your choice. Just asking them questions about what they will and won't do for your care should give you some enlightening answers about their style of practice. Personally, what I look for in a birth attendant is what Dr. Robert Bradley called "a wide behind, and the wisdom to sit on it."[56]

"None of the above" is also a possible choice, but unassisted childbirth is a riskier option, in more ways than one, and not one to undertake lightly, without considering all the what-ifs, both medically and legally.

Sometimes it makes more sense to pick the place of birth first, and then the provider. Most hospitals will let you take a tour, though you may need to schedule it ahead of time, or call before you come to make sure that they're not too busy. Make a list of questions to ask. If they show you a waterbirth tub, ask what percentage of laboring women there actually use it. If the rooms are nicely decorated, ask what equipment they are hiding in the cupboards, and when they will be using it. Ask how many mothers give birth without epidurals. Ask what their caesarean rate is. Ask whether they allow VBAC. Ask what the typical birth there is like. What monitoring do they require during labor? Do they have cordless monitors, so women have the freedom to move around? What may laboring women eat and drink? What options for pain relief do they offer; anything other than drugs? Take a look at their newborn nursery, and ask if newborns are required to go there, and if so, for how long. If they have an NICU (neonatal intensive care unit), ask what level it is, and what kinds of things they care for there. The more you know about the place ahead of time, the more you will know what to expect. Meet as many of the nurses as you can.

---

55 Placenta is high in vitamins, minerals, and the hormone oxytocin, which helps reduce postpartum bleeding, eases the hormonal transition from pregnancy to postpartum, triggers letdown of breastmilk, and promotes feelings of well-being and bonding.

56 I can't find the exact quote, but it is probably in *Husband-Coached Childbirth*.

## *Prenatal testing and screening, and newborn screening*

The part of prenatal care that is most related to frugality is all the tests and screens that are available these days. Here are some questions you might want to ask:

◆ Is it a test or a screen? (A test is a test, a screen is what they use to decide who should be tested.)

◆ What is it looking for? Or, what does a positive test result mean?

◆ What is my (approximate) risk of testing positive?

◆ What is the false positive rate? (How many positive test results are wrong?)

◆ What is the false negative rate? (How many of the negative test results are wrong? —The test results say you don't have it, when actually you do.)

◆ What is the ratio of false positives to true positives?

For many prenatal tests and screens, the chance of getting a false positive test result (one that puts you into a panic for no good reason at all—sometimes called the "nocebo" effect) is much greater than the chance of getting a true positive result. Even if you get a negative result, there is a chance that it is a false negative, and you really do have something you should be worrying about, instead of enjoying true peace of mind. Either way, the test will only tell you what it tells you, and then you have to decide what to do with it.

Many women prefer to avoid all this "prenatal scare", and skip most of the prenatal tests. Particularly the more invasive ones, such as amniocentesis and chorioamniotomy, which pose some risk to the life of the baby—even a perfectly healthy and normal one. Even the less invasive screenings can lead to intense pressure to go on to the riskier tests, to "know for sure". From piecing some research together, I have become convinced that the rate of miscarriage caused by amniocentesis[57] is slightly higher than the

---

[57] While the actual miscarriage rate from amniocentesis probably varies quite widely from practitioner to practitioner, the neonatal death rate also varies from midwife to midwife. Both of the averages are small, around 2 to 3 per 1000. When comparing homebirth statistics with hospital birth, remember that the homebirther population has disproportionate quantities of Caucasians, hippies, religious fundamentalists, refugees from hospital VBAC bans, medicophobes, multiparas (mothers of multiple children), grand multiparas (mothers of a whole bunch of children), and older mothers in general.

neonatal death rate for babies born at home with a midwife in attendance. Amniocentesis has become a very commonly offered procedure,[58] but it is actually just as dangerous as homebirth! (And it provides a stunning example of misperception of actual risk: do-it-yourself, and you must be crazy; let a doctor do it, and it must be safe. Except that you aren't, and it isn't.)

As for detecting problems before the baby is born, most things that will be found are conditions that you can't do anything about (other than abort) until the baby is born anyway. Even then, it might not be so bad. The mother and writer Barbara Curtis is taking care of *four* "Downzers" (three adopted), by the grace of God.[59] I have heard of *waiting lists* for people who wish to adopt Down Syndrome or other special needs babies.

You might as well learn about your newborn screening options now, too. After your baby is born, you will be asked to allow someone to take a few drops of blood out of the baby's heel. This blood will be tested for a number of diseases and genetic disorders. Some of them are quite serious, but they are generally also quite rare. Anyway, if the blood screens positive for anything, the Health Department will be tracking you down, pronto.

The issue with newborn screening is that many states keep the blood samples and test results for quite a long period of time.[60] Some keep them *indefinitely*. The samples are in some cases used for research. If you prefer to not leave a sample of your child's

---

58 The American College of Obstetricians and Gynecologists (ACOG) recommended in 2007 that all pregnant women be offered amniocentesis, for the detection of Down Syndrome (though the only "cure" that they can offer for this genetic abnormality is abortion, and some insurance plans will only pay for amnios for higher-risk mothers) and other conditions. The miscarriage rate from amniocentesis is also greater than the Down Syndrome detection rate—so, more healthy babies are being sacrificed than Down Syndrome babies are being "prevented", even before you take into account the false positive babies that are aborted.

59 She blogs at **http://mommylife.net/**

60 See the Citizens' Council on Health Freedom chart at **http://www.cchconline.org/pdf/50_States-Newborn_Blood_Retention_Policies_FINAL.pdf** for how long each state keeps newborn screening blood samples.

DNA[61] left in the hands of the government, you may have options for opting out of the screening, or of opting to have the blood samples destroyed. It depends on the laws of your state. Or you can have screening done by a private lab, but you will probably have to pay out of pocket.

"Am I done yet?"

# *Estimating the due date*

Due dates are not expiration dates, just a rule of thumb for when to expect the baby to arrive. For first babies, it's typically about 41 weeks (counting from the start of the last menstrual period). For later babies, gestation runs about 40 weeks. But normal term pregnancies can last anywhere from 37 up to 43 weeks. (A range of more than a month!)

Naegele's Rule (280 days from the first day of the last menstrual period, or 266 days from conception) is often used to estimate the due date, but it underestimates the actual length of gestation, by nearly a week for first-time mothers, and by about three days for other mothers.

# *Preparing for parenthood*

The first task in preparing for parenthood is to accept the pregnancy, and accept the changes in your life that it will bring. Spend some time grieving your old life—many

---

61 See the Citizen's Council on Health Freedom (at **http://www.cchconline.org/index.php3**) for more information about genetic privacy issues.

things that you have been accustomed to are going to change. Get ready to make some major sacrifices in your level of freedom to just do the things that you want to do. Let go of the need to get X hours of sleep per night—a baby will often need you in the middle of the night. Much of the sleeplessness of the third trimester is from your body preparing for a more flexible sleep schedule.

You are entering a new season of life. "You may be able to do it all, but not all at the same time," one wise person said.[62] After your children are grown, there will be another season of relative freedom. The childbearing and childrearing years will fly by faster than you think.

That doesn't mean to put *everything* off until menopause. Some things you will choose to make time for now, rather than postponing until your nest is empty. Don't squelch your natural talents and gifts so much that they burst out in a full-blown midlife crisis the minute your last child goes off to kindergarten. (Again, see *Women in Midlife Crisis*, by Jim and Sally Conway.)

Another thing to grieve is the loss of your old body. Pregnancy will almost certainly leave some permanent traces on it somewhere, if only a few stretch marks. As Ingrid Trobisch said in *The Joy of Being a Woman*,[63] "Every woman has to learn anew in every phase of her life to understand what happens in her body biologically and to live in harmony with herself." Also she wrote about the connection between self-acceptance and spiritual health: "If I do not live in peace with my body, I do not live in peace with my Creator."[64] Accept the biology of pregnancy, labor, birth, and breastfeeding, and what they will do to your body.

Then, look forward to who you want to be as a parent. Look back at your childhood, and try to learn from your parents' mistakes. Prepare to bond with your child—you can even start during pregnancy by talking to the baby.

Finally, take good care of yourself. And let others help.

---

62 See Chapter Four of *Women in Midlife Crisis*, by Jim and Sally Conway.

63 In *The Joy of Being a Woman,* page 4.

64 Ibid.

# *Maternity and nursing clothes*

## *Maternity clothes*

Most maternity clothes are just horrible: overpriced, ugly,and poorly constructed of the wrong materials; though they are not quite as horrible as they used to be. Stay in regular clothes as long as possible. Switching to plus-size clothing (instead of maternity clothes) is also horrible, the proportions are all wrong, even for plus-size women,[65] but at least you have the possibility of finding something that is not made of polyester.

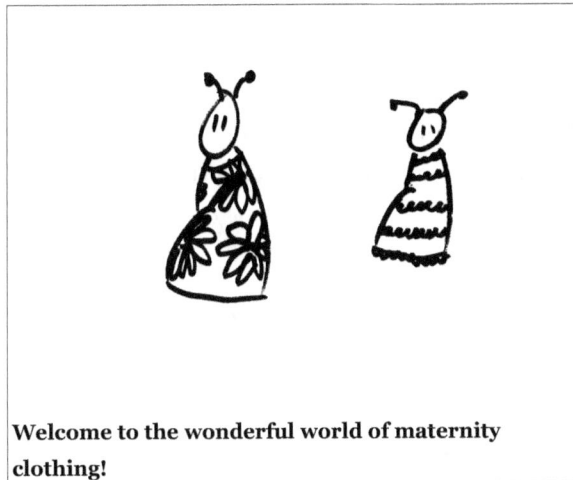

**Welcome to the wonderful world of maternity clothing!**

I very seriously advise against buying any maternity clothing made of polyester. If you are pregnant, you will naturally be too warm much of the time. And polyester is a terrible fiber to wear when you are already too warm. (Also a terrible fiber when you are too cold.) I know this from painful experience, because I wore a 100% polyester band uniform in marching band, from the heat of late summer into the first snows of winter. I roasted or I froze; there was no "just right". Believe me, polyester is always wrong. Cotton in the summer, and light wool in the winter (or just summer clothing, layered), are far better choices.

---

65 Barbara Deckert, in *Sewing for Plus Sizes,* explains why designers have a hard time designing clothing for anyone who isn't a fit model, and why the standard sizes and pattern shapes for plus-sized women really don't fit anyone.

Even when the fabrics are all right, most maternity clothes are still ugly in one way or another. Or simply too small—most maternity clothes seem to be made with tiny pregnant teenagers in mind.

So this is the time to invest in buying or making some size-adjustable clothes that will fit you at a variety of weights and shapes. A woman that is pregnant, and then postpartum, is not in a season of figure stability. This would be a good time to learn to sew, if you haven't yet—skirts in general are relatively easy to fit and sew, and a good way to start learning. Simple drawstring skirts are *very* easy to sew, and can be made large enough to fit through pregnancy. If you want a level hemline, you will have to add more length in the front, to account for the pregnant tummy.

For tops, my first choice is to borrow shirts from my husband. Men's shirts are made much longer than women's shirts, just what is needed to go around the tummy. At the very end of pregnancy, though, I have nearly outgrown even his extra-extra-large shirts. Then I am miserable, and ready to be done. Other women, who buy traditional maternity clothes, have also had the problem of outgrowing the largest sizes in late pregnancy.

Having to wear the same few maternity outfits over and over and over for months at a time is very tiresome. You might want to save one or two outfits to bring out in the last few weeks of pregnancy, just for the sake of morale. Then another new outfit or two, once the baby is born—it will take some time to get back to your pre-pregnancy weight (not to mention pre-pregnancy shape).

You will probably also need some new, larger bras. I went up two band sizes and at least one cup size with my first pregnancy. Maternity bras have extra adjustability, so you won't outgrow them as quickly, but you could also just buy a few thrift store bras as you go.

Pregnancy will probably leave you with permanently wider feet. That means you will need some new shoes, if you can find any in your new size.

For winter, layering is your best bet. Depending on your due date and location, you may or may not need a larger coat. I prefer to wear my usual coat, with an additional warm layer underneath to compensate for the fact that I can't zip it in mid-to-late pregnancy.

I have heard of maternity stores selling their mailing lists, so if you sign up for one, you could find yourself receiving a lot of mail (and coupons) from formula and diaper manufacturers.

## Nursing clothes

For nursing clothes, look for clothing that allows discreet access to the breasts. This usually means separate tops and bottoms; then you can at least nurse by pulling up the top. The baby will cover most of the exposed tummy. Otherwise, you can look for clothing with built-in nursing openings. Some companies, such as Motherwear,[66] specialize in making nursing clothing. The problem is that it is very difficult to design clothing that has workable openings which are not totally obvious when not in use, and that are stylish and comfortable to wear. Nursing clothes also have many of the same drawbacks as maternity clothes. The postpartum body has its own fitting problems.

If you can wear more than one layer, that gives you more options. I have done a lot of public breastfeeding wearing a converted T-shirt, with a button-down shirt over it. With my second baby, though, I usually just wear a regular, loose shirt, and pull it up in front.

This is how to convert a T-shirt (or similar knit shirt) to a nursing shirt:

1.  Mark where you want the openings to be; they need not be directly over the breast; placing them below and further to the side makes them easier to conceal with a button-down shirt or sweater.

2.  Cut the holes, which can just be slits.

3.  (Optional) Sew edges of holes to reinforce them, by whichever method you prefer. (I just leave the raw edges unsewn.)

Nursing bras are somewhat difficult to fit. Usually, the bra size that you need in the third trimester will be the same as the nursing bra size you will need. Avoid underwires, and anything that constricts breast tissue—this can lead to uncomfortable plugged milk ducts, which can in turn lead to painful breast infections.

Nursing bras and tanks have become much more widely available in recent years, in stores like Walmart and Target. So look for a slightly stretchy nursing bra, with either an

---

66 **http://www.motherwear.com/**

access panel or enough stretchiness to allow just pulling it down to expose the nipple. (I use sleep bras for my main nursing bras. ) Either way, you should be able to do this one-handed—your other arm will be busy holding a crying, flailing baby. Avoid bras with any scratchy fabric or lace—you may be on the inside, but the baby will be on the outside.

# 3

# Big Things I — Feeding

Most of the ongoing costs of a baby are concentrated in four areas: feeding, diapering, daycare (if you use it), and health care. You probably don't have much control over how much the baby's health insurance will cost. You do have some control over how much feeding the baby will cost you, but if you're going to save money by breastfeeding, you have to start right at the beginning.

### Breastmilk versus formula, and boob versus bottle

Babies were designed to eat breastmilk, for at least the first year or two. (This is what Baby Jesus ate, of course.) Formula is an adequate substitute for most babies, but it will never be as easy to digest, nor will it contain mom's antibodies against whatever germs are going around. Sick and weakly babies especially need breastmilk. The health benefits of breastmilk are being trumpeted at expectant mothers these days, *ad nauseum,* so I will skip over most of those. Here are some of the less well-known benefits of breast-feeding:

- ◆ Breastfeeding promotes "happy hormones" in the mother (oxytocin, the "bonding hormone", primarily), making her calmer and more mellow; the emotional attachment between the mother and the baby has a physiological component. As Ingrid Trobisch notes in *The Joy of Being a Woman*, the more the mother gives, the more she receives.

- The varying flavors of breastmilk prepare the child for eating a variety of solid food. (Formula always tastes the same.)

- Breastfeeding colonizes the baby's digestive tract with the right bacteria, from the mother's skin, which will greatly help in preventing diarrhea and other illnesses.

- Nursing signals the mother's body that there is a baby around, and that it should hold off on making any other babies for a while. It is possible to delay the return of periods and fertility for a year or more, and to naturally space the children a couple of years apart.[67]

- There is also a significant reduction in breast cancer risk. In one study, nursing reduced the risk of getting breast cancer by 59% for women with a family history of breast cancer (and so have the highest risk of getting it).[68]

- For older babies and toddlers, breastmilk (straight from the tap) is a lot less spillable than anything in a bottle or sippy cup. And if they are still nursing, you don't need to worry about their diet or picky eating habits nearly so much.

- The preparation and cleanup are minimal, which is especially helpful when traveling or living without a dishwasher.

Some of the benefits of breastfeeding seem to come from the baby being held close to the mother while nursing, and having that additional (and frequent) interaction with her. If you formula feed, you can hold your baby during feedings like breastfeeding mothers do. The antibodies in breastmilk are best delivered to the baby by nursing directly. So skip the breast pump whenever you can, and just feed the baby straight from the tap.

### Drawbacks of breastfeeding

Breastfeeding is a happy time for mothers,[69] and one of the great joys of womanhood, but nursing a baby does have some drawbacks. Getting started can be very difficult;

---

67 This doesn't work for everyone; some women seem to have irrepressible fertility.

68 According to a press release of recent research at **http://www.sciencedaily.com/releases/ 2009/08/090810161858.htm**

69 As Ingrid Trobisch describes in *The Joy of Being a Woman*.

breastfeeding seems to be a learned skill, and there are not nearly as many older women with breastfeeding experience around as there should be.

There is also often a lack of cultural support, starting right in the hospital. Many women avoid or curtail breastfeeding in order to go back to work, and nurses are no exception. They usually are the first ones to be available to give mothers breastfeeding help, yet are likely to have not breastfed long-term themselves (though some nurses are absolutely awesome, of course). Formula feeding is also much easier for nurses to assess and chart. Doctors and pediatricians (and even certified lactation consultants) also frequently display remarkable ignorance about breastfeeding, and regularly dispense misinformation about it. The real breastfeeding experts are the mothers who have breastfed their children.

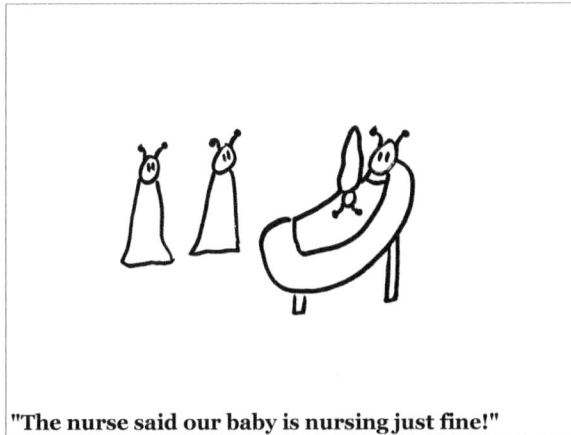

"The nurse said our baby is nursing just fine!"

The six-week maternity leave is another enemy of breastfeeding: most babies hit a growth spurt right about then, and want to spend a lot more time nursing. Breastfeeding beyond the maternity leave will require either drastically cutting back on work hours (and income), or a solid commitment to spending a lot of time with the breast pump.

Pumping has its own drawbacks: it is practically as much work to pump as it is to breastfeed directly—in some ways, it is more work—but you don't get to hold and cuddle the baby. The increasing cultural support for pumping is more for the benefit of employers, government, and providers of pumping supplies and childcare than for mothers and babies.

Nursing restricts your clothing choices to clothes that keep the breasts fairly accessible. Most nursing clothes are as horrible as maternity clothes.

Breastfeeding maintains higher levels of some of the pregnancy hormones. So if you are breastfeeding, pregnancy gingivitis can persist all the way to weaning.

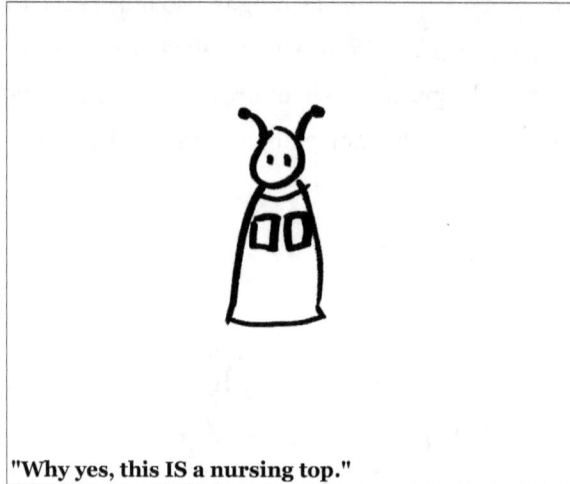

**"Why yes, this IS a nursing top."**

Finally, breastfeeding can simply be painful, awkward, and downright annoying. Even a baby with a good latch will cause sore nipples some of the time. Nursing discreetly with other people around is a skill that takes self-confidence and practice. Sometimes I get touched out, and resentful of having to make my breasts available to the baby. It is no fun when the baby reaches out and grabs a fistful of nipple, or chomps down with their sharp new teeth. But these things pass, and pass quickly: "It came to pass—not came to stay," says Barbara Curtis in *The Mommy Survival Guide*.

## Ecological breastfeeding and the Lactational Amenorrhea Method

Ecological breastfeeding is hardcore breastfeeding. The mother satisfies all the baby's needs for suckling and nourishment, day and night. The main things are to:

- Keep the baby close to mom day and night.
- Feed on demand around the clock.

- Allow comfort nursing.
- Avoid pacifiers and breastmilk substitutes.
- Nurse lying down for a nap, if possible.

To effectively suppress fertility, by what is called the Lactational Amenorrhea Method, these guidelines (basically the same as Ecological Breastfeeding) should be followed:

- Keep the baby physically close.
- Baby fed on demand; no nursing schedule.
- Baby sleeps close to mom and feeds several times a night.
- No pacifiers; allow the baby to comfort nurse.
- No supplementation or bottles; all baby's nourishment is from the breast.
- Wait until six months of age to introduce solid foods, then do it slowly.
- Mom needs to eat well and take time to rest, for good milk production.
- Mom's periods have not yet returned.

As long as periods have not returned, this method is 99% effective in preventing pregnancy for the first six months, and about 94% before the first period. The average return of periods for ecologically breastfeeding mothers is at about fourteen or fifteen months; between nine and twenty months is normal. (The first few cycles may not be fertile ones, especially if they return early.) So it is a free (other than a rather large opportunity cost) and easy way of spacing children eighteen to thirty months apart.

Pumping for work, and feeding the baby breastmilk by bottle during the day, seems to reduce the effectiveness of LAM somewhat, because there is less, and less frequent, breast stimulation.

Abrupt changes in nursing pattern may hasten the return of fertility.[70] It is not usually necessary to wean to get pregnant again.

Ecological breastfeeding sounds a lot harder than it actually is. Remember that nursing builds up levels of bonding hormones in the mother, and helps her feel centered and

---

70 There is a good introduction to ecological breastfeeding and LAM at
**http://www.kellymom.com/bf/normal/fertility.html**

loving. The rest is just ditching all the things that get between a mother and a baby. Your baby needs you, so keep them close and nurture them.

The delay in return of periods is one huge benefit of ecological breastfeeding. It is very helpful to not have to deal with PMS, or with painful menstrual cramps, while taking care of a little baby.

## Not so hardcore breastfeeding

I suppose it is possible to not feed totally on demand, on sort of a loose schedule. But I can't endorse any feeding routine that advises you to watch the clock, rather than watching the baby.

It does seem like some babies who are left with another caregiver will eat far less frequently for a while, and then make up for it later in the day when mom returns. Some babies hardly eat at all during the day in daycare, and then nurse all night with their mom—"reverse cycling". (My baby did that, too, just because he was very busy during the day playing with his newfound freedom to scoot across the floor and explore new things.)

Mothers who try to schedule nursings typically try to make sure that the baby eats a full meal at every feeding, rather than a little sip 'n' snack. This gets more difficult as the baby gets older and more distractible.

People who supplement with formula, or pumped breastmilk, probably get the best, along with the worst, of both worlds. My guess is that it is difficult to do in the long term: the paths of least resistance will tend to lead to one extreme or the other, and more likely toward exclusively formula feeding. Still, any breastmilk for the baby is better than none, and even partial breastfeeding is a significant accomplishment.

## Pumping

Pumping is a compromise between the needs of the baby, and outside demands on the mother. It is not really any easier on the mother: she still has to make the milk, and deliver it. All it does is get her out of feeding it directly to the baby. Pumping itself is no fun, but some mothers who can't breastfeed directly manage to exclusively pump for their babies for months, or even years.

Some states have laws encouraging businesses to make accommodations for breast-feeding mothers to take pumping breaks; the health care reform bill requires larger employers to provide time and space for pumping breaks. It is worth looking into exactly what your state's laws are. On the other hand, many jobs that aren't pumping-friendly are also so low-paying that you might as well save the money on daycare and other work expenses and stay home.

Jury duty may create another situation in which it is necessary to pump. Some states have laws that exempt breastfeeding mothers, or people who care for their small children or provide other sorts of caregiving, from jury duty.[71] My state, alas, does not, although at least some districts have formal or informal policies that allow nursing mothers to defer jury duty. If you are breastfeeding and called up for jury duty, go ahead and ask to be excused. I did, and received a one-year deferment (less than I asked for). However, the next year, I had to haul the hated breast pump down to the courthouse and serve my time. The courthouse staff was fairly accomodative; in the jury pool, I could sign out and go to the "mother's lounge" (a small windowless room with a chair, table, and electrical outlet). When I was on a jury, I told the judge that I would need pumping breaks, and was able to pump in a conference room during the regular courtroom breaks. Don't be afraid to ask for what you need. If you need to rent a breast pump solely for jury duty, ask for reimbursement (although it will probably be denied).

The use of used consumer breast pumps is discouraged, because pumps tend to create less and less suction as they age, and also because some models can harbor bacteria from the previous user within the machine.[72] (Hospital-grade pumps are designed to accommodate multiple users.)

In looking for a pump, check on the reliability of the pump model, what additional parts you may need to purchase, and how it is powered (cord or batteries or manual). Hospital-grade pumps are best when there are problems with low milk supply, but if breastfeeding is going well, a standard pump is sufficient. If you are only going to need a pump for the short term, they can be rented fairly inexpensively—though you may have

---

71 State-by-state information on jury duty exemptions for caregivers is available at Family Friendly Jury Duty's website: **http://www.familyfriendlyjuryduty.org/**
72 Somehow this is more of a problem than the bacteria from you is.

to ask around to find out where they are available. Insurance will sometimes cover all or part of the cost of buying or renting a breast pump, if you have a prescription from your doctor.

Stay-at-home moms who rarely leave their babies can use a manual breast pump, or just hand express milk. These methods are slow, though. *Baby Bargains* says that the mini electric pumps are also slow, and have weak suction.

You will also need containers for storing breastmilk; plastic bags are the most popular option. Plastic or glass bottles are sometimes preferred, though: some research showed that antibodies and leukocytes from the breastmilk stick to the bags (more than to bottles), and don't get to the baby. (So if you need a cheaper option, use small glass jars—leave extra room for expansion if you are freezing them—instead of Ziploc® bags.) You may also need some way of keeping pumped milk cold, if it is going to be more than ten hours before you can get it home (assuming room temperature of about seventy degrees; four to six hours for hotter temperatures). Freezing breastmilk destroys some of the antibodies, so fresh breastmilk is best.

Pumps that allow you to pump both breasts at once, but require you to use both hands to hold the pump flanges in place during pumping, are incredibly inconvenient. One mother made a hands-free double pumping bra by cutting holes in a sports bra.

## *Nursing pads*

Sometimes lactating breasts leak milk. Nursing pads, which are placed in the bra to soak it up, can be either reusable or disposable. It is easy to sew reusable ones out of flannel scraps. I have some disposable ones that I have never used in two and a half years of breastfeeding. Honestly, I just go without them, except for very special occasions, since I usually wear multiple layers in public, and very rarely leak enough to soak through them all. When you have a baby, you will get spit up on regularly, not to mention the occasional runny noses and diaper containment breaches. Compared to those, breastmilk is no big deal. It washes right out.

## *Nursing covers*

Nursing covers are optional; if using one makes it easier for you to breastfeed, that's great. The biggest problem with them is that babies like to try to fling them off. The second biggest problem is that when you use one, it is pretty obvious to everyone that you are feeding a baby under there. (For real stealth nursing, look as much like your normal self as possible, and pretend that the baby is sleeping. This is hard to pull off when the baby is kicking and waving his arms.) For a nursing cover, a light receiving blanket or baby afghan will do. Remember that the baby needs to breathe under there!

## *Nursing pillow*

A nursing pillow is most useful in the early days of nursing, when the baby is small, and needs a boost up to the breast. There are special nursing pillows, such as the Boppy®, and then there are the regular pillows that you already have around your home. Sitting in chairs that have arms will reduce the need for pillows.

## *Formula*

The basic composition of formula is regulated by federal law, so the generic brands are just about as good as the pricey ones, which keep inventing new ways of making formula "as good as breastmilk". The powdered formulas are the least expensive.

Breastfeeding mothers get all the good formula coupons and formula samples, so if you are planning to formula feed, it is worthwhile to have a friend who is going to breast-feed, and due around the same time that you are, or to pretend to be a breastfeeding mother yourself when you create a baby registry or sign up for a mailing list. Formula companies market much more heavily to breastfeeding mothers, because once they start using formula, they have more brand loyalty, and also bottlefeed for longer than mothers that started out with formula.

For supplementing with formula because of low milk supply, remember that the only way to increase breastmilk production is with extra breast stimulation, preferably from a hungry baby. While some formula may be necessary, it will work against building up a good milk supply. As one of our friends has told us, "You get better at the things that you do."

## Bottles and nipples

It is probably worthwhile to find the most breast-like bottle nipples that you can, to simulate the sucking motions of breastfeeding, since it has a definite influence of the development of the palate and jaw—babies that breastfeed end up needing orthodontic work less often in adolescence.

Some people prefer to use glass baby bottles, to avoid any chemicals that might leach out of plastic bottles. Some of the used plastic bottles around these days will not be BPA-free, but new ones should all be.

Holding the baby during feedings as breastfeeding mothers do is good for the baby. Remember, too, that formula pooling around the teeth too often will lead to tooth decay.

## Bottle warmers and sterilizers, and washing bottles

Bottle warmers are not really necessary; room temperature is good enough for the baby. (At least that is what I've heard.) Sterilizing bottles is not generally necessary, either— the dishwasher is good enough. For handwashing bottles, you will need a bottle brush, and then just give the bottles a good wash and rinse in hot water and a little dish soap, and then air dry. (I think I would give them an extra hot rinse, myself, to get any remaining soap residue off.)

## Formula costs

The cost of formula varies from baby to baby, depending on how much they eat, and which kind of formula they use. Denise and Alan Fields, in *Baby Bargains*, say that formula will cost about $759 for the first six months,[73] just for the powdered stuff.

---

73 Eighth edition, page 246.

# 4

# Big Things II — Diapering

The essential characteristics of a diaper are: comfortable, securable, changeable, soaks up urine and contains poop, disposable or washable. Both the cloth and disposable diaper camps have a multitude of options. For most of my diaper-changing career, we have used a mix of homemade prefold cloth diapers, and cheap disposable diapers. But now we only cloth diaper our children: I was tired of throwing our money away!

One thing you should know about cloth diapers is that they are bulkier, and won't fit under all of today's baby clothes. It takes a little more effort to find baggier clothes that accommodate a cloth diaper. Most daycares also won't touch cloth diapers. Diaper rash creams are difficult to wash out of cloth diapers.

The biggest difference I have found is that cloth diapers require a little more thought. When we were using both cloth and disposables, I would frequently use disposables just because I was tired, and didn't want to think about it. But now that cloth diapering is my only option, it has become much easier to do.

Even if you choose to exclusively cloth diaper, it's a good idea to keep some disposable diapers around, in case of an emergency where you can't wash diapers for a few days. Since disposables are quickly outgrown, and true emergencies are rare, the most frugal option is to make a stash of emergency diapers out of old clothing or inexpensive thrift store fabrics (or at least to keep a stash of such fabrics available for ad hoc diapering). Soiled diapers can be stored in plastic garbage bags, and either thrown away or washed after things return to normal. Old flannel receiving blankets make good no-sew emergency diapers.

## *Cloth options*

It might surprise you to learn that cloth diapers are not all that messy or stinky. A good diaper cover will contain the mess, and cloth diapers don't have the chemicals that make dirty disposable diapers so terribly smelly. The poop of breastfed babies doesn't smell bad. Having used both kinds of diapers in a side-by-side comparison, I can tell you that the cloth diaper pail can get a little stinky, but even if I go away for two weeks on vacation and let it sit in the summer heat, it will never get as bad as the disposable diaper pail gets after only one or two days. (We use a dry pail for cloth diapers, which I will explain below.)

Cloth diapers range from the all-in-one (AIO) diaper, which integrates the cover with the diaper, to various pouch-and-insert systems, to prefolded diapers, to flat diapers—simple squares of fabric that you fold into a diaper. Some diapers have built-in snap or Velcro® fasteners.

There are also variations on the fabrics used, from fleece to microfiber to suedecloth to flannel to birdseye textured cotton to cotton knits to PUL (polyurethane laminated fabric) to wool to hemp and bamboo. Fleece and microfiber and suedecloth (all of which are polyester) wick away moisture, flannel is absorbent, birdseye dries quickly, cotton in general is inexpensive and easy to find and easy to wash thoroughly, PUL is waterproof and yet can withstand the heat of the dryer, wool is breathable yet fairly waterproof and antimicrobial, hemp and bamboo are absorbent and have some antimicrobial properties.

Here are the main styles of cloth diaper:

- ◆ **All-in-ones** are fairly expensive, because they require more sewing, and much more sewing skill. Also, they take longer to dry than prefolds or flat diapers. Since the diaper and cover are together, there is no option to let a damp cover airdry, and then reuse it without washing it. Also, if the elastic gives out, after many cycles through the washer and dryer, the diaper is basically done for. Unless you buy used ones cheap, or sew them yourself, they are not very frugal.

◆ **Foofy diaper systems**: what pieces you have, and what you do with them depends heavily on the diaper system. Pockets, stuffings, liners, covers; there is a lot to learn. They can get quite expensive, unless you can find used ones for sale (people often try to recoup some of the high initial costs), and they definitely have a steeper learning curve. However, people dedicated enough to figure them out often swear by them.

◆ We use **prefolds** that I have sewn from old towels and flannel sheets. Prefolds have two layers of fabric, with extra layers sandwiched in the middle for absorbency. I made three sizes: small for newborns, medium for crawlers, large for walkers. The prefolds that you may be able to find in the stores, usually of birdseye cotton, are considered by cloth diaper connoisseurs to be inferior in quality and absorbency, but other people say that they work just fine. (Prewashing them multiple times before the first use will help make them absorbent.) There were once many links to free diaper patterns online at The Diaper Hyena; now defunct.[74] (I largely followed the prefold pattern of Confessions of a Cloth Diaper Fanatic.[75]) The one thing I don't like about the prefolds I made is that the flannel dries stiff and "crunchy" if I only airdry them. I do like the various flannel prints that I found: some with flowers, some with leaves, some with snowflakes, some with paisley, some with stripes. My children have colorful diapers!

◆ **Flat diapers** are what my own mother used on me; they are versatile, easy to wash, quick to dry. By learning different folds, you can customize the fit as your baby grows. Double them up for larger babies. There are a number of different folds, which all basically fold the diaper into a triangle or a narrow rectangle—sometimes with an added twist at the crotch—which covers the baby's bottom and is pinned (or hooked with a Snappi®) in place.

◆ **Diaper service?** There are now two diaper services in our large metropolitan area. For a while there were none, as rising gas prices made diaper delivery

74 **http://www.thediaperhyena.com/reap.htm** [Currently available, unfortunately—Dec. 2010]

75 Currently at **http://webpages.charter.net/rhamley/diapers/diapertext1.htm**

unprofitable. Diaper services vary on whether or not they will allow you to use your own diapers, and they are rather expensive, but quite convenient. Used but still usable diaper service diapers are sometimes available, at a reasonable cost.

- ◆ **Diaper doublers** are thick pads made of several layers of diaper fabric, that can be added to the crotch area of a diaper, to increase absorbency. These are especially good for cloth diapering on the go, and at night.

- ◆ **Diaper liners** are thin pads (sometimes only a single layer of fabric) that can be added to the crotch area of the diaper, to keep the messy stuff from being mashed into the diaper too much. Sometimes these are fleece or microfiber, to wick moisture away from the baby, but synthetic fibers can be harder to wash, and harder on the baby's skin. There are also disposable diaper liners. I've cut rectangles from old T-shirts, to use as disposable cloth liners while traveling.

### Diaper covers

Diaper covers for prefold and flat diapers can be anything from felted-wool "soakers" or "butt sweaters", to fleece versions of the same, to the old-style nylon pants with elastic edges (which can be hard to find these days; too low-tech), to plastic-lined material with Velcro® fasteners...to I don't know what. Just don't use plastic bags—they are a suffocation hazard to the baby. We use a mix of different kinds of covers.

**"Just how many layers are on this baby's butt?!"**

Wool soakers can be made of shrunken old sweaters, or knitted or crocheted from wool yarn. Technically, wool covers should be given a little lanolin before use (to repel moisture), and handwashed, but I don't do either. From what I've read, the way to do it is to melt a little lanolin (Lansinoh®, the lanolin cream for sore nipples, is the easiest way to buy it) and add it to a sinkfull of water, with a tiny bit of soap. Swish the (clean) covers around, squeeze them in a towel to remove excess water, and lay them out to dry, without rinsing.

How many diaper covers to have: as many as the number of times you expect your baby to poop between washings, plus a good many more in case of diarrhea or other tummy upset. Newborns poop often, sometimes as often as they are fed, which can be a dozen times a day; older babies and toddlers usually poop one to four times per day (at least mine have).

All diaper covers can be handwashed. Most covers can be machine washed right along with the diapers, but most shouldn't go through the dryer—hang them to air dry instead. I do put some of my least favorite homemade recycled-sweater soakers through the dryer, because I can easily replace them. (They wear out much faster because of the heat and the tumbling action.)

### Making a diaper cover from an old wool sweater

This is how I make wool diaper covers from old wool sweaters that don't fit well anymore. This style of cover works best for babies who aren't very mobile yet; more active babies tend to wiggle their way out.

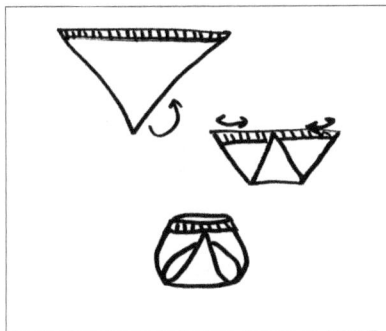

1.  The optional first step is to felt the wool first, in or out of the washer. Give it a good hot wash, with a little wool wash detergent, and something to agitate against (such as an old towel that you won't mind getting wool fibers on)

and then a good cold rinse. Dry it in the dryer if you want. If you don't want to felt it, then after cutting out diaper pieces, stitch along all the raw edges to keep the knitted fabric from unraveling.

2. Next, measure the baby's waist.

3. Now, cut equilateral triangles out of the sweaters, with each side being the same length as the baby's waist measurement, and trying to have one side be along a hem or ribbing (this will be the waistband of the diaper cover).

4. Bring up the crotch point of the triangle, and stitch to one of the side points, leaving enough of it open for a leg hole. Then repeat on the other side.

5. Turn the cover right side out and you are done!

## Diaper fasteners

There are also choices in diaper fasteners. Diaper pins, the Snappi® (a Y-shaped fastener with hooks on each end), plain old Velcro® tabs, or snaps that you set yourself. Some diaper covers secure the diaper well enough that a fastener isn't even needed. Most of the time I use diaper pins. They are simple, and they work. Some of our diaper pins are ones that my mother used. I have never poked a baby with one, though I have poked myself a time or two. (I keep my finger along the pin to keep the baby off it.) A couple of pairs of diaper pins will do; you only need two at a time. They are getting harder to find; we were able to find some at the grocery store.

Ordinary safety pins aren't strong enough (or safe enough) for long-term diaper duty, and they will rust, which makes them very difficult to push through the diaper fabric.

## Cloth wipes

If you are going to use cloth diapers, you might as well use cloth wipes, too. We used cloth wipes even when we were using only disposable diapers. We have a variety: some old/cheap washcloths, some flannel squares, some terry cloth squares, some flannel on one side and terry on the other (easy to sew—see below). It's nice to have a variety of wipe options available. We wet the wipes with near-room-temperature water from the bathroom. Some people make their own special wipe solutions. Some people use cloth wipes for the whole family, in place of toilet paper. That is a little too extreme for me.

### Sewing two-sided cloth wipes

This is terribly easy sewing—easier than sewing a potholder, really:

1. Cut two squares of equal size, one of terry cloth (old towel), and one of flannel (old receiving blanket or sheet or nightgown or whatever).

2. Place the "good" sides together, and sew around three of the edges, plus just around the corners onto the fourth side.

3. Turn the wipe right side out, tuck the last raw edges in, and sew the opening closed.

4. (Optional) Topstitch around, along the edges of the entire wipe; this keeps it from turning in on itself in the wash.

## *Diaper pail*

We had a surprisingly difficult time finding a good diaper pail for cloth diapers. Amy Dacyczyn in *The Complete Tightwad Gazette* says that any good pail with a tight-fitting lid will do. We looked all over town for a plastic bucket with a reusable lid that you could get on and off without too much trouble, that was not too easy for an older baby to open, and that would stand up to being opened and closed several times a day for months on end. No luck. Finally, we ended up ordering a diaper pail with a latching lid online. We bought a bucket of birdseed for a disposable diaper pail, and used it for over a year.

We might have done better to ask around at bakeries or restaurants for empty food-service buckets. Other people have recommended a wastebasket with a tight-fitting lid. We didn't think at the time that that would provide enough odor containment; now I think that it would, for a dry pail system. Which I should now explain....

Dry pail versus wet pail: In a dry pail system, the dirty diapers and cloth wipes are just placed in a diaper pail, with no extra water. In a wet pail system, the diaper pail contains a diaper soaking solution—water with some borax added, usually, that helps clean the diapers while they are waiting to be washed. But you have to keep the pail away from the baby, as it is a drowning hazard. With a dry pail system, people usually substitute an extra wash, in cold water, in place of the soak. We use a dry pail, ourselves.

Shaking the loose poop off the diapers into the toilet before putting them into the dia-per pail is a good idea (though not strictly necessary if there are no large lumps). Some may need to be scraped off. An old spatula will do. I use an old ice scraper. The rest of the poop will come out in the wash. The poop of breastfed babies isn't really stinky, or much of a problem to wash out. Some people rinse diapers out in the toilet, by taking a firm hold on the diaper, and dipping it in the toilet as it's flushing—not very effective with modern water-conserving toilets. There are also special diaper sprayers that con-nect to the toilet's water line, which some people find very helpful.

## Cloth diapering at night, and on the go

Cloth diapering at night presents an additional challenge. Preventing leaks is difficult, and even many hard-core cloth diapering parents resort to putting disposable diapers on their babies at night. And the same when taking the baby out and about.

The keys to getting through the night without leaks seem to be to provide sufficient absorbency, by using a diaper doubler of some sort (special doubler pad, folded newborn diaper, or simply using a larger diaper for the extra bulk), and paying special attention to the diaper cover, and to tucking the diaper into the cover properly. I reserve my best covers for night, and for going out.

When out and about with cloth diapers, bring a "wet bag" to bring the dirty diapers home in. You can buy a special nylon bag or two for this (they can be washed along with the diapers), or you can just use a plastic bag.

## Washing diapers

Only a small amount of detergent is needed for washing diapers, because the ammonia from the urine in them will do a lot of the work. You can disinfect diapers by hanging them in the sun, by boiling them, or by bleaching as explained below.

There are even more different ways to wash cloth diapers than there are kinds of cloth diapers. The basic method that we learned was:

1. Store dirty diapers in a dry pail.

2. Do one cold wash with a little detergent and some enzyme cleaner (such as Biokleen®, which I omit nowadays).

3.   Do one hot wash with a little more detergent, and ½ cup (8 fluid ounces) of white vinegar in the rinse cycle.

4.   Add an extra rinse at the end.

This method recommended washing diapers at least every other day, but we got by with washing diapers twice a week, and even with only doing a single wash and rinse, though it is not exactly ideal. (Remember that most diaper services only wash diapers once a week.) Less frequent washing means that you will need to buy or make more diapers, so you don't run out. It is recommended to not wash more than two dozen diapers in a load, so that they have room to move around and scrub each other in the washer. Loads that are too small are also harder to balance in the washer (for a top-loader). If you have a high-efficiency washer, have it add more water for diaper washing, if you can. The vinegar in the rinse water helps the diapers to smell fresh and clean. If the washer does not have a fabric softener dispenser (for the vinegar)—as our coin-operated apartment washer does not—you can put the vinegar in a Downy® ball and throw it into the wash.

For a time, when we were using mostly disposable diapers, I washed the cloth wipes only once a week,  with a single hot wash, and ½ cup of vinegar in the rinse. Cloth wipes spend much less time in contact with the baby's bottom than diapers do, so skimping on the wash is less likely to result in diaper rash.

For a wet pail system, pour off the soak water into the toilet, or just pour everything into the washer and run it through a spin cycle before washing. (This pouring business doesn't work well at all when there is a bag lining the diaper pail—the soaking water goes everywhere. ) Then go straight to Steps 3 and 4:  a hot wash with an extra rinse.

In the old, old days, apparently dirty diapers were immediately rinsed, left to soak (probably with the soak water changed daily), thoroughly washed on wash day, boiled on the stove, and then hung to dry.

If your baby gets a lot of diaper rash, it could be that the diapers aren't getting clean enough, and that it's time to modify your diaper washing method.

The use of chlorine bleach for diapers is somewhat controversial.  Some people say that the chlorine will react with ammonia in the urine, and cause terrible diaper rashes (chemical burns, really). Other people wouldn't dream of washing diapers without disinfecting them with bleach. My conclusion, after giving it some thought, is that I would never use bleach without soaking (and draining) or washing the diapers first. Dirty diapers contain a lot of urine, the urea in the urine gets broken down into ammonia by bacteria, and bleach and ammonia should *never* be mixed. So get the ammonia out first. Then, after bleaching, rinse the diapers thoroughly.

### Detergents for cloth diapers

The best detergent for diapers, so we were taught, was regular cheap, unscented detergent that was not soap-based. Soap can leave a film on diapers that reduces absorbency and reacts with urine to produce an unpleasant odor. Probably this is more of a problem in areas with hard water. The residue can be stripped off as outlined in the next section. There are special detergents for baby things, but they are more expensive, and not necessarily any better than the simple cheap detergents.

Some people say that homemade laundry soap (often based on Ivory®, Zote, or Fels Naphtha® soap) is okay for diapers, but when I tried it, it did leave some residue .

### Stripping cloth diapers

If cloth diapers are not absorbing well, or they have a funny odor after being washed, or they keep giving your baby diaper rash—possibly from picking up soap residues left over from other loads, or from bacteria lurking in the middle of the diaper—try stripping them. Simply  run the diapers through a hot wash with a little hand dishwashing detergent (such as Dawn®; the original blue stuff seems to work the best) added. Or boil them in a big stockpot on the stove (but watch it closely to keep it from boiling over). Or see if the nearest diaper service will strip them for you.

## *Drying diapers*

Diapers can be dried in the dryer, on the hottest setting (but take out the diaper covers containing nylon or plastic or wool and hang them up) or hung up to dry, preferably outdoors in full sun so that the sunlight can disinfect them and fade away the stains. I run mine through one dryer cycle, which leaves them slightly damp, and then hang them up indoors. Someday I will have an outdoor clothesline of my very own.

# *Disposable diapers*

Disposable diapers seem to fall into two camps: the Over-Engineered, and the Almost-Too-Skimpy. The Over-Engineered diapers have all the bells and whistles. I am sure that it is only a matter of time before they come out with a solar-powered diaper that contains genetically engineered bacteria that will convert all the baby's pee and poop into a small lump of dry, inert matter that smells like strawberries. This diaper will also contain a GPS unit, which will automatically sync with your cell phone, in case you ever misplace your baby. And the diaper will only need to be changed once a week. Which is good, because it will cost around $300 for the base model, bacteria starter kit, and software installation—software normally provided by the baby not included.

In the meantime, the Over-Engineered diapers tend to fit babies well, do a fairly decent job containing messes (most of the time) and still need to be changed at least several times a day. If you're going to buy this kind of diaper, be sure to buy the ones with the right licensed characters on them; you will probably be paying a few cents per diaper just for the pictures on it.

The Almost-Too-Skimpy diapers are the cheap version, they open and close and more or less fit, and absorb and contain just about as well as the Over-Engineered kind, for half or two-thirds of the price.

In any case, you may have to try a few brands to find one that works well for your baby, one that fits well at the legs and waist, and also absorbs enough. Putting a disposable diaper on a baby is just as much of a learned skill as cloth diapering is; it may take some time for you to figure out how to minimize leaks.

Be careful when comparing diaper costs to compare by cost per diaper. The number of diapers in a package decreases as the diaper size increases, but older babies need diaper changes less often. Also, heavy wetters may have to switch to the next larger size before reaching the listed weight range on the box. Disposables are cheapest when purchased in large quantities.

## Disposable wipes

We have only used the cheap disposable wipes, and then only in the diaper bag. They are pre-moistened, but they are more effective if you wet them down with water before you use them. I find that they are too small, and don't lift off poop nearly as well as cloth wipes do, so I wind up using many more of them.

For the more expensive wipes, really it would be cheaper to buy a few yards of on-sale fabric (or use rag bag fabric that you have on hand) and cut it up to make *disposable* cloth wipes. We live in a time where fabric is often less expensive than paper.

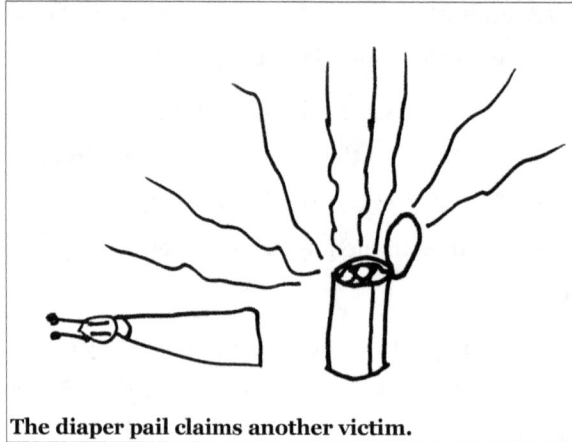

**The diaper pail claims another victim.**

## Wipe warmer

I use cloth wipes dampened with tap water. If the tap hasn't been used for a while, then the wipes and water are both near room temperature, and my babies don't mind. Once in a while, though, the baby gets an ice-cold wipe. They really make a face then!

Wipe warmers got a bad reputation a while back, when some of them were recalled as a fire hazard. They also can use up to fifty or sixty dollars worth of electricity per year (assuming electricity costs of 8 or 9 cents per kilowatt hour, and leaving the warmer on all year).

## Diaper pail for disposable diapers

The Diaper Genie® dominates this market, and for good reason: used disposable diapers stink to high heaven. My cloth diaper pail might really reek of ammonia, but I've never staggered away from it muttering, *"This smell is going to kill me!"* I did not have a Diaper Genie®, only a pail with a tight-fitting lid, and it was no fun to open it. That is one of the big reasons that I gave disposable diapers the boot: I got hit by that smell at every diaper change, and again when I took out the trash. I expect that the bag inserts for the Diaper Genie® are pricey.[76] Supposedly dropping or scraping the poop into the toilet will help reduce the smell, but most disposable diaper users choose disposables because they don't want to deal with the poop.

One of the competing disposable diaper pails allows you to provide your own bags. Most of the rest of them are just plastic buckets with tight-fitting lids, unless you want to spend a lot of money on a stainless steel trash can (which doesn't absorb odors like plastic does).

## Comparing costs: cloth versus disposables

There are many variables in cloth diapering costs and disposable diapering costs, so there is no one-size-fits-all answer as to which is cheapest. *Baby Bargains* says that cloth diapers (with a diaper service and covers that you buy) can run from $850 to $1200 per year. They don't give an estimate for the cost of cloth diapering if you buy diapers and wash them yourself, but they do estimate that cloth diaper and cover costs can range from $200 to $880.[77] Those prices can easily be beaten. Generally, cloth diapering is the cheaper option, as long as the cost of the diapers and the laundering is not too high. The following is my best stab at calculating actual cloth and disposable diapering costs.

### Cloth diaper calculator

There are a lot of variables involved, because there are so many ways to cloth diaper. I will use my own case as an example.

Start with the cost of the cloth diapers themselves:

\_\_\_\_\_Number of diapers

---

76 According to *Baby Bargains*, refills cost about $100 per year.

77 Eighth edition, page 198.

X_____Cost per diaper

=_____Cost of diapers

I have about sixty cloth diapers (in three sizes) that I sewed myself, at a cost of about $25 for used flannel (sheets, nightgowns, receiving blankets), terry cloth (old towels), and thread.

Cost of diaper covers:

_____Number of covers

X_____Cost per cover

=_____Cost of diaper covers

We have a variety of diaper covers: about a dozen wool covers in various sizes, cut from felted old sweaters; these cost $10 at most. We have six nylon covers in a newborn size that I bought at a rummage sale for $2. We have one toddler-size cover that I found at a yard sale for 25 cents. We also bought some new covers, four with Velcro® for about $8 each, and two nylon ones for $5.50. So my total cover cost has been about $56.

Cost of diaper fasteners:

_____Cost of fasteners

A pack of four diaper pins costs about $2. Two per baby is enough.

Cost of cloth wipes:

_____Number of wipes

X_____Cost per wipe

=_____Cost of cloth wipes

Most of my wipes were made from flannel and terry scraps left over from making diapers, plus a few older washcloths that I had. So my cloth wipes were basically free.

Diaper pail:

_____Cost of diaper pail

We bought a diaper pail, and two nylon bags to line it, for about $50 online.

Now, add these all up:

_____Diapers

+ _____Fasteners

+ _____Covers

+ _____Wipes

+ _____Diaper pail

= _____Up-front cloth diaper costs

This gives you the up-front cost. My up-front cost was about $133. I included my toddler diaper costs in this, because I made most of my toddler diapers at the same time as the newborn and medium-size diapers. Some of the covers we bought as we needed them. I could use a few more nylon covers.

I left out the number of hours that I spent sewing diapers and wipes—a prefold diaper, from start to finish, took me about 45 minutes. I could make a two-sided wipe (flannel and terry) in five or ten minutes. A wool diaper cover takes about five minutes to cut and sew, once the old sweater is purchased and felted.

Next, there are the costs of washing the diapers. The first variable is how often the diapers are washed. Some people wash every day, and other people stretch it out and only wash once a week. Ideally, I would wash diapers three times a week, but usually I only wash twice. So:

_____Loads of diapers per week

Cost of running the washer (ideally, I would do two full washes, cold then hot, plus an extra rinse at the end, but with coin laundry I just do one hot wash):

_____Number of washes per load of diapers

X _____Cost per wash (may include cost of water if you pay for water)

= _____Cost of running the washer

It costs me $1.25 per load to use the apartment building's laundry. When I had my own washer, it cost less than $0.50 to run the washer. (I haven't figured the cost of additional wear and tear on the washer, probably less than $1 per week. Two or three extra loads a week is not that much; many families wash ten or more loads a week even without washing diapers.)

Cost of detergent:

_____Cost of detergent per small load

My detergent costs about $14 for an 80-load box, or 5 cents per load. I would divide a small load's worth in detergent between the first wash and the second, if I were doing two washes per load.

Cost of vinegar (I put white vinegar in the final diaper rinse):

_____Cost of ½ cup vinegar per load of diapers

Vinegar costs about $2 per gallon here, each gallon has 16 cups, so a half-cup costs about 6 cents.

Cost of drying diapers:

_____Cost per kW·hr, figuring that diapers take an hour to dry, and running a dryer with electricity takes about 1000 Watts (or 1 kW).

My drying cost is $1.25 per load, and it leaves them damp enough that I have to hang them up to finish drying. (Cost of wear and tear on a dryer should also be around $1 per month, if you want to include it.) Sometimes I hang the diapers to dry, but this makes them stiff and less absorbent.

So, putting it together:

_____Cost of running the washer

+ _____Cost of detergent

+ _____Cost of vinegar rinse

+ _____Cost of running the dryer

= _____Cost of washing and drying a load of diapers

I added mine up, and I get $2.61. It would be much less if I had my own washer and dryer.

Now, multiply by the number of loads per week:

_____Cost of washing and drying a load of diapers

X _____Loads of diapers per week

= _____Cost of washing and drying diapers per week

In my case, $2.61 multiplied by two is $5.22.

Then, figure cost per year:

_____Cost per week

X    52 weeks in a year

= _____Cost of washing cloth diapers for a year

My cost per year is about $272.

Add the up-front costs, and you have the cost of diapering and washing diapers for the baby's first year:

_____Up-front cost of diapers, covers, wipes, diaper pail

+ _____Cost of washing cloth diapers for a year

= _____Cost of cloth diapering for the first year

For me, $133 up-front costs plus $272 washing costs equal $405. But the diapers and covers and wipes and diaper pail will last much longer than one year. I suppose I could try to amortize the costs, but this will do for a first-pass analysis. This is less than half of the *Baby Bargains* estimate of the cost for a diaper service.

Cloth diapers do occasionally leak and cause extra regular laundry, but so do disposables. Badly soiled baby clothes can go in the diaper pail and be washed along with the diapers.

## *Disposable diaper calculator*

Cost of diapers per year:

_____Cost of diapers per week

X    52 weeks per year

= _____Cost of diapers per year

For us, this number held steady at about $10-$15 per week. Smaller babies will go through more diapers, but larger diapers cost more. Figuring $12.50 on average, our cost was $650.

Cost of disposable wipes:

_____Cost of wipes per week

X    52 weeks per year

= _____Cost of wipes per year

If we didn't use cloth wipes, we would probably go through one box of disposable wipes per week, which would cost about $2, or $104 per year.

Cost of special trips to the store to buy diapers:

_____Miles to store

/ _____Miles per gallon (gas mileage)

X _____Cost of gasoline per gallon

X _____Trips per year

= _____Cost of special trips

We usually bought diapers twice a month at Target, about 5 miles round trip to the store, gas costing about $2.50 per gallon, 20 miles per gallon gas mileage. So at least $16.25 per year, plus time spent in the store.

Cost of diaper pail and bag refills:

_____Cost of diaper pail

+ _____Cost of bag refills per year, which is: _____Cost of bag refill  X
                              _____Number of bag refills per year

= _____Diaper pail costs

In our case, we bought one pail of birdseed at $7 for the bucket, and used no bags.

Cost of disposing of diapers in the garbage:

_____Cost of garbage bags, if needed

+ _____Additional cost of garbage removal per year

= _____Cost of diaper garbage per year

We spent about $5 extra per year on garbage bags, because disposable diapers created more garbage, that had to be taken out more frequently. It has not cost us anything for the additional trash removal.

Add it up:

_____Cost of diapers

+ _____Cost of disposable wipes

+ _____Cost of going out to buy diapers

+ _____Cost of diaper pail and bag refills

+ _____Cost of diaper garbage

= _____Cost of disposable diapers per year

My total is about $782 (higher than the *Baby Bargains* range of $400 to $500[78] because I included costs of wipes, diaper pail, shopping, and disposal), and we went very cheap on the diaper pail. So in my case, using cloth diapers cuts my diapering costs in **half** the first year, and even more after that (because I can keep using the diapers). If I had my own washer and dryer, or an outdoor clothesline, the savings would be even more dramatic. My "hourly wage" for sewing diapers, wipes, and covers was $4.50 an hour for the first year, and has gone up to about $10 an hour, now that I am on the third year of using them—because I figure that the value of the time I spent sewing increases the longer I use the cloth diapers and wipes in place of disposables.

## *The third way: Elimination communication*

There is actually a third diapering option, one that you can use in conjunction with either cloth diapers or disposables: elimination communication. The basic idea is that you observe your baby, to find out their patterns of peeing and pooping. Then, when it is about time for them to go, hold them (securely, so they feel safe) over a bucket or the toilet, and make a cue noise (such as "pssss") to cue them to go. This actually works for some people. While little babies can't be expected to "hold it", apparently they can be trained to release on cue, starting at about three or four months of age.

I have only made brief attempts at teaching my babies elimination communication, and I found it difficult, because I work from home, tend to get absorbed in my work, and am not attentive enough to when the baby goes, or is about to go. But it is a easy, no-cost technique that is worth giving a try.

Jean Liedloff describes something even more extreme (from a Western point of view) in a primitive tribal setting, in *The Continuum Concept*:

> When [the baby] wets or defecates, [his mother] may laugh, and as she is seldom alone, so do her companions, and she holds the infant away from her as quickly as

---

78 Eighth edition, page 198.

she can until he finishes.  It is a sort of game to see how fast she can hold him away, but the laughter is louder when she gets the worst of it. Water sinks into the dirt floor in moments and excrement is cleared away immediately with leaves.[79]

Hmm...if I had a dirt floor, I wouldn't need to vacuum, either.

---

79 Jean Liedloff, *The Continuum Concept*, page 55.

# 5

# Big Things III and IV — Daycare and

# Health Insurance

I won't have a lot to say about these topics, but I'll tell you what I know.

## *Daycare*

I haven't used daycare for my children. If I had to get daycare, the first thing I would figure out is what level of care I wanted. Some daycares offer a lot more than others. My personal preference would be to choose an in-home daycare with a smaller number of children, or even a full-time babysitter: they will have more continuity of care with their care provider, and will see much more daily home life, rather than a more artificial institutional environment. The more that children can get out and interact with a variety of people and a variety of settings out in the real world, the better. I think that academics for young children are very much overstressed; partly, I suspect, to salve parents' guilt at handing their children off for so many hours at a time.

Here are some more questions I would ask:

◆ What do they teach in the way of essential living skills? (Such as teaching babies how to safely climb stairs.)

◆ How many children per staff member?

- How do they structure the day? How much flexibility is there if your child isn't quite with the program?

- What do they supply, and what do you have to supply (food, diapers, etc.)?

- Where does this particular place fall on the cost spectrum, and why?

- Do you like the staff that you meet?

- Do you feel like you can trust these people with your child day after day?

- Is their childcare philosophy compatible with your parenting philosophy?

For a bigger place, you will probably also want to know about their check-in and check-out procedures, security and so on. You want your baby to be there when you go to pick them up!

Any daycare should have a license, and insurance, and employees who aren't criminals, and so on, if you want to check into it really thoroughly.

Also, I would look for an attitude of respect for the parents and parental authority. They may be experts on children in general, but you are the *de facto* expert on your particular child, and ultimately responsible for the child's upbringing. You are also the customer who is paying them for the service.

If you want something cheaper than daycare, you have few options besides getting free childcare from a friend or relative, or working opposite shifts from your partner. One-on-one care for your child is almost always going to be more expensive than more institutional care.

Many parents these days have to cobble together multiple sources of childcare, and settle for less than ideal care situations. Our cultural support systems have not kept up with our cultural mandates.

## *Health insurance*

While Congress passed the Obamacare health bills (Patient Protection and Affordable Care Act and the Health Care and Education Reconciliation Act) in April 2010, there's probably not a lot that you can do right now about your health insurance. Big changes are being phased in over the next few years, but for most people little has changed yet. If you get health insurance through an employer, then your choices are limited to the plans that they offer. If you are on government aid for health care, you are probably stuck until you get a job that offers health insurance benefits. If you are self-employed or purchasing health insurance on your own for some other reason, health insurance costs you an arm and a leg, and you pay for it with post-tax income. For the formerly uninsurable, health care reform is bringing new high-risk pools, but these vary by state, have not gotten off to a good start in many cases, and are seriously underfunded.

The one thing we did, before our second child was born, was to switch to a high-deductible health plan (HDHP) with a health savings account (HSA), through my husband's employer. This lowered our premiums so that we are paying about the same now, for the four of us, as we were paying for the three of us before. We are quite healthy, and have a health savings account to help us cover the high deductibles. (The employer threw in a big contribution to the HSA, as a incentive to switch. This was one factor in our decision.) Once the deductibles are met, the HDHP covers a higher percentage of costs than the old plan did, so it is the better option if we get very sick, too. (I should add that since our second child was born in the early spring, and we were using an out-of-network midwife, our insurance wasn't going to pay for much for that pregnancy, no matter which plan we chose.)

The main benefit of a high-deductible plan, besides providing catastrophic coverage, is that the things that you do pay for out-of-pocket are billed to you at the insurer's customary rates (for in-network providers, at least), so you pay less than you would if you were uninsured, or totally self-insured. The health care reform is bringing major (and unwelcome) changes to HDHP/HSA coverage, however, as you will see below.

## Health Care Reform

To prepare for writing this section, I skimmed through both of the health care reform bills; an arduous task. I don't claim to understand it all, but the following are my conclusions, and to the best of my knowledge they are correct. I've given references to specific sections of the legislation wherever possible.

The first bill, over nine hundred pages long, is HR 3590, the Patient Protection and Affordable Care Act of 2010 (PPACA). This is where almost all the meat is. The second bill, HR 4872, is the Health Care and Education Reconciliation Act of 2010 (HCERA).[80] It is much shorter, roughly fifty pages, and contains mainly amendments to the first bill, along with measures for student loan reform.

Most of the provisions of these bills are being phased in gradually, from 2010 to 2015. I believe that this transition is going to be messy, simply because of the complexity of the legislation. The new law is not only difficult to decipher and understand, but much of it consists of line-by-line amendments to earlier laws, such as the Public Health Service Act, the Social Security Act, and the Internal Revenue Code.

The basic requirement, so far as the taxpayer is concerned, is the establishment of a requirement to purchase health insurance, under penalty of law, beginning in 2014.[81] Subsidies are provided for some, in tiers based on income relative to the federal poverty line, but there is also a tax penalty for not purchasing qualified health insurance: once phased in, it will be up to $695 per year for an adult, and half of that for a minor—and both will be adjusted henceforth for inflation. Initially, the penalties are $325 in 2014,[82] and $350 in 2015. Taxpayers and their dependents must be insured for every month of the year to avoid a prorated penalty. There are some provisions for waiving the penalty for those who cannot afford premiums, who are in hardship, or who are in various other circumstances. Health insurance plans are required to report who they insured, and for which months of the year, to the IRS.

To be considered qualified health plans under the law, health insurance plans will have to cover quite a bit[83]:

- Basic preventative health care, such as physicals and vaccinations.
- No exclusions based on pre-existing conditions—including pregnancy—which will bring many people out of uninsurability.[84]

---

80 Full text of both bills can be found via the Library of Congress at: **http://thomas.loc.gov/**

81 PPACA, Section 1501; addition to Internal Revenue Code of 1986, as amended by HCERA, Section 1002.

82 This is far as I can tell from HCERA Section 1002, which amends PPACA Section 1501 in a way that either contains a typo, or is beyond my comprehension.

83 PPACA, Section 1302.

84 PPACA, Section 1101.

- Waiting periods for new insurance to kick in will be limited to 90 days.[85]

- Deductibles are limited to $2000 for individuals, and $4000 for families (with adjustments for inflation), for employer-sponsored plans.[86]

- Elimination of lifetime limits on benefits, for qualified health plans; annual limits on benefits cannot be unreasonably low.[87]

- Catastrophic-only coverage will be limited to individuals under the age of 30, minors, and some who are in economic hardship.[88]

The system of group health insurance plans mainly organized by employers will remain, but each state will also set up an insurance exchange to facilitate individual purchases of health coverage.

Existing health care plans will be grandfathered in,[89] but their continued existence will depend on insurance issuers continuing to offer them, and on employers continuing to offer them to employees. Additionally, some of the above requirements, such as limits on waiting periods, removal of lifetime limits, and requirements to allow enrollment of dependents to age 26 will (or already do) also apply to grandfathered plans.[90]

## Cost-cutting

A major purpose of the health care reform legislation is to bring health care costs down. It will force young, healthy people to purchase coverage—paying much more in premiums than they receive in care, in order to subsidize the care of the not-so-healthy and the formerly uninsurable. It also makes substantial changes that will cut Medicare costs for caring for the elderly. Since Medicare already reimburses health care providers for less than the actual costs of caring for the elderly, it is likely that further cost cutting will only result in poorer medical care for the aged.

---

85 PPACA, Section 1201, in the addition of Section 2708 to Public Health Service Act.

86 PPACA, Section 1302.

87 PPACA, Section 1001, addition of Section 2711 to Public Health Service Act.

88 PPACA, Section 1302.

89 PPACA, Section 1251.

90 HCERA, Section 2301.

The legislation requires insurers to cover regular preventative care, in the hopes of saving money by reducing the incidence of expensive health problems in later life. It also attempts to greatly reduce the number of uninsured people, whose unpaid health care costs are passed on to the insured population as higher fees for services.

The reform has several unpleasant implications. For one, the option of making insurance affordable by purchasing high-deductible health insurance and saving for health expenses in tax-free accounts is being severely limited. Secondly, the level of coverage mandated by the law is likely to be almost unaffordably expensive, despite the promised subsidies and caps on premiums. Third, the law limits the amount that insurers can adjust premiums based on health risk factors and age, which will drive up premiums for the younger and healthier population. And the option of forgoing insurance entirely and self-insuring will put you in the position of paying almost as much in penalties as you would for health insurance, without receiving any benefit at all from it.

For most people, the pressure to reduce health care costs is going to produce a distinct downgrading of medical care and care providers: nurse practitioners instead of doctors for routine care, nurse-midwives instead of OBs for many pregnant women (as is already happening in some areas because of OB shortages), and so on. The bills devote many lines to measures[91] meant to improve the health care workforce by training new providers—few of whom will be doctors.

Also, to reduce health care costs, we can expect to receive much more nagging about healthy lifestyle choices, from the federal government on down. For example, being overweight, defined as a Body Mass Index (BMI) greater than 25 (which is only borderline overweight, if that, depending on the individual; more than half of American adults have BMI > 25), is defined in the legislation as a "chronic condition" for Medicaid purposes,[92] requiring special care. There will also be more encouragement from health insurers and employers to participate in wellness programs, because of cost pressures and federal incentives—and as one of the few options provided in the legislation for reducing one's own health insurance costs.[93]

---

91 PPACA Title V, for example.

92 PPACA, Section 2703.

93 PPACA, Sections 1201—addition of Section 2705 to Public Health Service Act, and PPACA Sections 4303 and 10408.

The legislation provides for a huge increase in data sharing between federal and state agencies, including state vital records, employment records, and tax records, for determining initial and continuing eligibility for government health care programs.[94] The Internal Revenue Service will also be provided with information on everyone's insurance status, from health insurance issuers and from larger employers.

New internet portals for health care and health insurance information,[95] more transparent statistics on hospitals and physicians, and simplified application processes for government health care programs[96] will be helpful for many people. But the provisions for automatically enrolling eligible children and adults into government and employer health care plans (including the CLASS Community Living Assistance Services and Supports program[97]), on an opt-out basis rather than an opt-in basis, may be more help than some people are looking for.[98]

The legislation also creates considerable headaches for health care and insurance providers.

## Implications of health care reform for women

One significant effect of health care reform is that health plans will be required to provide maternity coverage. Currently, many plans exclude pregnancy entirely, or on the basis of being a pre-existing condition. Also, women can be covered under their parents' health plans until age 26 (though their own children could not be, and would probably be covered under Medicaid or CHIP).[99] In the transition period, group plans are

---

94 PPACA, Section 1561.

95 PPACA, Section 1103, for example.

96 PPACA, Title II, Subtitle C.

97 PPACA, Title VIII, see in particular the addition of Section 3204 to the Public Health Service Act.

98 PPACA, Section 2202, amendment to the Social Security Act allows hospitals to make preliminary determinations of eligibility for Medicaid. See PPACA, Section 1511 for automatic enrollment into large-employer plans (with opt-out available).

99 PPACA, Section 1001, addition of Section 2714 to the Public Health Service Act. It's not entirely clear whether this includes married women or not; HCERA Section 2301 attempts to clarify (unsuccessfully) by removing "who is not married" from Section 2714.

required to enroll adult children under the age of 26 who do not have access to an employer-sponsored plan themselves.[100]

Additionally, the legislation is paving the way[101] toward a much more midwife-based model of care,[102] with certified nurse-midwives (CNMs) providing primary care for most pregnant women. CNMs are simply less expensive than OBs, thus reducing health care costs for low-risk pregnancies. While I personally prefer midwife care, I think everyone should be free to choose for themselves. Most American women prefer OBs, for their advanced medical training and their experience in handling complications. Also, busy CNMs in a clinic setting cannot provide the level of one-on-one care that I receive from my independently practicing midwives.

There are some interesting specifics in the PPACA which I believe show the way the wind is blowing in maternity care: first, it authorizes Medicaid payments to freestanding birth centers (which are defined in an unusually broad way as not your own home, and in compliance with state laws).[103] Secondly, it authorizes CNMs to make home visits, for providing maternal health and prenatal care services to Medicaid clients.[104] I expect that these practices will eventually trickle up into the privately insured population, similar to how Britian's National Health Service provides midwife and health visitor services. I also believe that the reform's provisions for training up more health care workers[105] will be used to train a great many more CNMs.

---

100 HCERA, Section 2301.

101 See, for example, PPACA Section 3114, which apparently increases the Medicaid reimbursement for CNM services.

102 While the United States ranks relatively low in birth statistics, such as neonatal death rate, compared to countries with socialized medicine and midwife-based maternity care, there are two important things to realize: first of all, the U.S. has a much more racially diverse population than the European countries it is compared to. Second, the U.S. makes aggressive efforts to save extremely premature babies (born at 25 weeks, or even earlier) that other countries may not even count as live births. So the statistics are not telling the whole story, by any means.

103 PPACA, Section 2301.

104 PPACA, Section 10605.

105 PPACA, Title V.

The legislation also creates the "Maternal and Child Health Bureau", and the "Administration for Children and Families", from which we can no doubt expect many new regulations and policies.

There are also initiatives aimed at helping improve maternal oral health, and at assisting mothers who are students or who are victims of domestic violence or abuse.[106]

### Implications of health care reform for children

The reform requires insurance companies that offer PPACA-compliant coverage to also offer child-only plans.[107] Catastrophic-only child coverage will also still be available.[108]

Qualified health plans must offer coverage for children that is at least as good as the state insurance program.[109] Children without other coverage may be presumptively determined to be eligible for Medicaid at (and by) the hospital.[110] Coverage for vaccines is mandated for qualified health plans.[111]

Longer-term, I expect that there will be initiatives directed at reducing the incidence of prematurity, to reduce health care costs—caring for preemies is incredibly expensive, and extremely premature babies have very high rates of death and permanent disability.

### Implications of health care reform for families

Much of the subsidies for health care premiums depend on family income relative to the federal poverty line.[112] Households with incomes that are up to four times the federal poverty line[113] may qualify for a tax credit. The tax credit is calculated as the difference

---

106 PPACA, Sections 10211-10214.

107 PPACA, Section 1201, addition of Section 2707 to the Public Health Service Act.

108 PPACA, Section 1302.

109 PPACA, Section 10203.

110 PPACA, Section 2202.

111 PPACA, Section 1001, addition of Section 2713 to the Public Health Service Act.

112 PPACA, Section 1401, addition of Section 36B to the Internal Revenue Code of 1986, as amended by HCERA, Section 1001.

113 Poverty lines depend on family/household size; the Department of Health and Human Service's 2010 poverty guidelines (which are formulated based on 2009 data) are $18,310 for a family of three, and $22,050 for a family of four.

between the premiums for a basic qualified health plan (one that is locally available, but not necessarily the plan that the household members are enrolled in) and a percentage of household income. The percentages run from 2% for a household under 133% of the federal poverty line, to 9.5% as a maximum. (These percentages are effectively caps on household premium costs; they are not the amount of the tax credit. The percentages may be adjusted later on to reflect trends in premiums.)

There are changes to the rules for FSAs and HSAs. One that takes effect in January 2011 is that these savings accounts may no longer be used for over-the-counter, non-prescription medicines, except for insulin.[114] There is also, beginning in 2013, a much lower limit to contributions to these accounts: $2500 a year.[115] And the penalties for using these funds for non-allowed expenses have been increased from 10% to 20%.

There are also tax implications, beyond the headaches of additional paperwork and computation. There are extra taxes for couples with incomes over $250,000 a year (and individuals with income over $200,000).[116] The itemized deduction for medical deductions has been decreased,[117] and the amount of health care premiums for which the taxpayer will receive a premium tax credit is no longer deductible.[118] Employer contributions to employee health care costs are now to be listed on each employee's W-2 form.[119] Some of the better health care plans will even be taxed.[120]

Younger parents may still be covered under their parents' insurance until age 26 (end of the month containing the 26th birthday), or under a child-only plan until age 21, but neither will cover their own children—these would most likely be covered under Medicaid or CHIP.

---

114 PPACA, Section 9003.

115 In the PPACA, this was scheduled to begin in 2011 as well, but HCERA amended it in Section 1403 to 2013.

116 PPACA, Section 9015.

117 PPACA, Section 9013.

118 PPACA, Section 1401, addition of Section 36B to the Internal Revenue Code of 1986.

119 PPACA, Section 9002.

120 PPACA, Section 9001.

Employers are not left unscathed. Health care costs are partly borne by employers, and the reform has significant compliance costs. Probably many companies will cease to offer health benefits, and elect to pay the penalties instead.

## Conclusion on health insurance

As it has been said before, "Health coverage does not equal health care!" Health care reform will extend coverage to nearly everyone, but the overall quality of health care provided is bound to decline. In short, pretty much everyone is going to get screwed, in one way or another, by the health care reform. I expect that its flaws will force it to be overhauled within a few years of its full implementation, and that the result will bring us considerably closer to fully-socialized, single-payer health care—the government taking over health coverage for everyone.

# 6

## Baby Equipment and Supplies

Everyone has their own list of must-haves and don't-needs. What ends up on your own list will depend a great deal on the temperaments of both you and your baby.

### *Philosophical considerations*

Don't waste money buying baby things that you will never use. Don't spend too much money on the things you do buy. But a calculated splurge is not wasteful. Alexandra Stoddard tells[121] how she admired, but could not afford, some exquisite baby bedding with hand-scalloped edges. But she saved and scrimped enough to be able to buy a single small baby pillowcase, which she used and used, and kept long after her babies were grown. That purchase was money well spent for her.

Babies grow extremely fast; many things they will outgrow in a matter of months, if not weeks. So finding "the best" of everything is not necessarily all that important. Anyway, this book is not about which name-brand manufacturers are the best for each item; *Baby Bargains* and *Consumer Reports* are better resources for that. Instead, I will tell you some creatively frugal ways to get everything you need for the baby, and options besides paying thousands and thousands of dollars for brand-new stuff.

---

121 In one of her books; I haven't been able to find the reference.

One variable that you have little control over is your baby's temperament.  You might get a few clues to your baby's personality while pregnant, but for the most part you will have to wait until the baby is born to meet them and discover what kind of temperament they have.  So you might well postpone some purchases until after the baby is born and you have a better idea about what they will like and dislike.

Frugality should not be dreary.  Even when money is tight, there is plenty of good, quality used merchandise in this country.  The thrift stores are full to overflowing, and perfectly good stuff is thrown away by the ton every day.  Most used stuff has actually seen some use, and you can see how well it has held up so far.

Prudent use of money is important, but so is a woman's urge to nest.  The nesting instinct is a biological imperative, so you

### The Chilling Effect of CPSIA

The Consumer Product Safety Improvement Act (CPSIA) was passed in August 2008, in response to a series of scandals involving safety hazards from imported toys.  Widely lauded as a big step forward in ensuring the safety of American children, the implementation and enforcement of the CPSIA law have gotten off to a rocky start; the Consumer Product Safety Commission officially postponed enforcement of many of its provisions.  The worst part of this law is that *any* seller of a children's product containing illegal amounts of lead may be fined up to $100,000.  Many thrift stores, including Goodwill, have opted to stop selling used children's merchandise entirely, rather than risk being caught selling noncompliant items, or having to screen thousands and thousands of unique used items for lead content.  So now there are fewer options for finding affordable used children's clothing, and used baby gear.

might as well make some allowance for it.  I do think, though, that this urge can be satisfied by cleaning and rearranging as much as by buying.  Instead of going on a spending spree and decorating a nursery from top to bottom, it might be wiser to do all the deep cleaning and organizing that you won't have time or energy to tackle after the baby is born.  Pregnant women have X-ray dirt vision.

Anyway, developing a good eye for quality will help you spot the real bargains.  Pay attention to these factors:

- Form and design:  Is it well-designed?  Pleasing to look at?
- Materials:  Is it made of quality materials that will last, and are not too difficult to care for?

- Construction: Is it put together well, and sturdy?

- Condition: Is it still in good shape? If not, is it repairable? By you?

There is no shortage of used goods in this country; with the average number of children per family running just over two, nearly all baby things will be outgrown before they wear out. While CPSIA is making (and will increasingly make) it more difficult to obtain used baby stuff, for now the supply is much greater than the demand, and you can save a ton of money by choosing used hand-me-downs over new.

## *Sources*

Where do you buy baby stuff? Here is a list of places to look:

- Start with the free stuff: hand-me-downs, FreeCycle, Craigslist, crisis pregnancy center (if you really need the help), or borrow from friends and family.

- Yard sales, rummage sales: Keep an eye on the ads in your local newspaper, and keep your eyes open for sales or signs while you are driving around.

- Secondhand store: thrift store, consignment store, re-use center, pawnshop: These are good places to look around, but beware of

---

**Lead Paint**

Lead paint can cause brain damage. Most lead poisoning these days is caused by flaking paint that exposes old lead paint, dust from painted surfaces that rub together, lead in the soil, or lead in metal parts or paints in children's toys and clothing. Lead is present in many flexible plastics and vinyls as a plasticizer. A flake of lead paint the size of a postage stamp contains enough lead for a fatal dose. If there are risk factors for lead exposure in your home, your doctor might want to do one or two lead tests in the baby's first year. The capillary blood test is less painful, the venous blood test is more accurate.

Blood lead levels that were perfectly normal back in the days of leaded gasoline and legal lead paint are now grounds for a personal visit from the Health Department. Typically they start to worry when lead levels exceed 5 or 10 µg/dL (micrograms of lead per deciliter of blood), because even these small amounts of lead have been shown to cause measurable damage to children's developing brains.

recalled items and items with lead paint and a lack of modern safety features. Expect decreasing levels of inventory of children's products, thanks to CPSIA (see sidebar earlier in this chapter). Even antique stores can be good places to shop, if you are looking for sturdy solid wood furniture, as long as you are aware of safety requirements.

◆ Warehouse club, discount store: Places with lower prices in exchange for a lower level of customer service, and with products packaged in truly enormous quantities. The downside is that you need extra storage space, and cash to tie up in purchased goods, as well as paying the membership fees. Their prices may or may not be better than regular stores' sale prices.

◆ Big-box store, department store: Watch for sales and clearance items.

◆ Boutique: Cute, but expensive!

◆ Online stores: Most of your baby stuff you should be able to find locally, and save on shipping costs. Save online buying for the things you can't find; for us, it was a good diaper pail for cloth diapers. We went crazy running around town trying to find a simple plastic bucket with a reusable lid, and ended up buying one online.

Now, how do you find these kinds of places? Start with the Yellow Pages, look under "Thrift", "Resale", "Consignment", "Surplus", and every other category that you can think of. Ask around, and see if your thriftiest friends and relatives will reveal the locations of their favorite "fishing holes". Take different routes when you are driving around town, and keep your eyes open. The good thrift and surplus stores tend to be in the same lower-rent areas as cheap (but good!) ethnic restaurants.

---

**A Note on Recalls**

The lists of safety rules for baby products is very long, and even reputable manufacturers frequently discover safety problems requiring mass recalls. There are dozens and dozens of recalls of baby stuff every year. So it is worthwhile to send in the product registration cards for your new baby equipment, and, if possible, to check the Consumer Product Safety Commission (CPSC) website at **http://www.cpsc.gov** for announcements of items that may have been recalled, and for safety checklists.

**In any case, look over both new and used baby items with an eagle eye for safety.**

Be sure to create an "exit strategy" for excess baby items. They take up a lot of space! Donate them to charity, sell them on consignment, hold a yard sale, or just give them away to a random stranger through FreeCycle, when you are done with them.

# Baby Stuff:  Little things

Remember:  babies grow fast; prioritize spending on things that will be useful beyond the first year, or that can be reused for the next child.  But also, some purchases can be delayed a lot longer than you might think—you can save yourself a lot of money and trouble if you wait until the time is right.

## Buying a house

Many people buy a house for the first time, or move to a larger house, to have more room for their baby.  "Can I afford to buy a house?" is almost as broad a question as "Can I afford to have a baby?"  The short answer is that if you can't afford to make a down payment of at least 20 percent, and keep your debt-to-income ratio at least below 40 percent, then you can't really afford a house.  Probably the smartest financial decision that my husband and I have made together was to stick to those two criteria during the housing boom.  We avoided buying a house that we couldn't really afford in the first place, and that we would have lost a lot of money on trying to sell after the housing crash.  As for now (December 2010), anyone who says that housing prices have bottomed out is clearly wrong (and probably is either trying to sell you something, or keep you from panicking over the state of the economy).  Many people say that paying rent is throwing money away, but being stuck with a house, unable to sell it or refinance because your mortgage is underwater, or losing absolutely everything that you paid on a house to foreclosure, is no fun either.

Anyway, babies don't really care how big your living space is.  All they care about being reasonably close to mom and dad.  They won't miss having a nursery, if you can't fit one in.  You can put off buying a house until the prices fall to a more reasonable level, and until you can save up a better down payment.

When you do buy a house, don't buy the wrong house—it can be an extremely expensive mistake. Buying and selling houses have huge transaction costs. Do lots of research on the house, and the neighborhood, and the community (including its prospects for long-term employment), before committing yourself to buying. Don't overlook the city ordinances and/or the homeowners' association (HOA) community rules—they may prohibit certain frugal practices, such as drying clothing on outdoor clotheslines. Also check into the neighborhood crime rates—these affect your cost of living, indirectly if not directly. Living in a less desirable area in a generally affluent zip code can lower both your housing costs and your car insurance rates significantly. Christopher Alexander *et al.*, in *A Pattern Language*, says that people are happiest when they live with people of their own subculture.

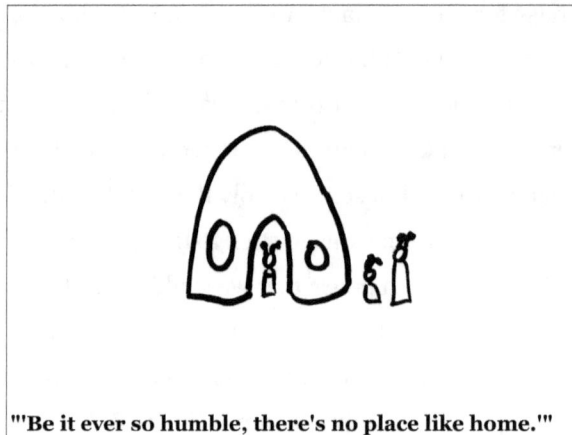

**"'Be it ever so humble, there's no place like home.'"**

If you are expecting to move within a few years, it will be smarter to rent rather than to buy. I know all about the nuisances of renting, after being a renter for the past fifteen years. Renting does make it much easier to move (and also sometimes more necessary—because that's often the only thing that you're allowed to change about your home).

Carefully consider the layout of spaces in the house, how one room flows to another; this matters more than square footage does. So do the layouts of storage spaces and kitchen work areas. Color is much easier to change than shape is. One light switch in the wrong place can add up to hours of annoyance, over the years.

If the baby can sleep in a room near the kitchen (or wherever you are spending most of your baby-free time), then you can probably get away without getting a baby monitor.

Christopher Alexander *et al.* also said in *A Pattern Language* that for a park to be usable on a daily basis, it has to be within three minutes of the home. I agree; we have a playground right outside our apartment, yet with the stairs and doors between us and the outdoors, just outside is almost too far away.

You can compute a "walk score"[122] for an address, to see what businesses and public areas are within walking distance, and how easy they are to get to.

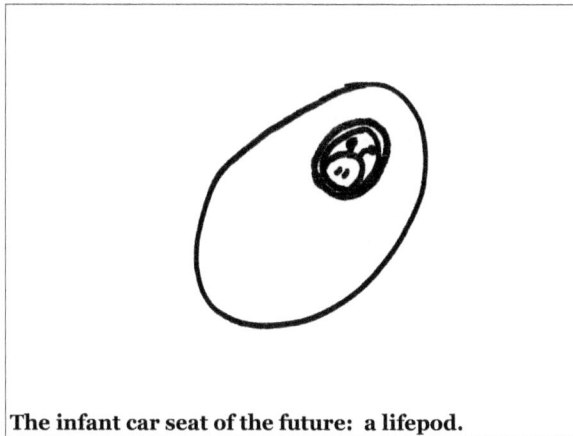

**The infant car seat of the future: a lifepod.**

## Buying a car

For driving your child around, all you need is a fairly reliable car with a backseat where you can install a car seat. Most people don't really need to buy a larger car or a minivan until the third or fourth child—in some cars it is impossible to install three car seats across.[123] If you wait, you can save up and greatly reduce (preferably to zero) the amount

---

122 Using the walk score calculator at **http://www.walkscore.com/**

123 The Car-Seat.org forums are a useful resource for answering car seat installation questions, in particular questions about how to squeeze car seats three across in specific car models: **http://www.car-seat.org/**

of car loan that you will need to take out.[124]  One rule of thumb is that the price of a car should not be more than one-fifth of your household's gross annual income; a similar rule said one-tenth—but perhaps they were thinking of a two-car household.

Buy a used car rather than a new car; it will have had many of the bugs shaken out, and it is much more affordable.  Again, do lots of research before buying, because this can yield a very high "hourly wage".

Having two cars per household is not absolutely necessary.  We only have one; it can be done.  It helps that we live close enough to my husband's place of work that I can drop him off at work and pick him up when he's done, on the weekdays that I need the car.

## Nursery

A nursery for the baby is completely optional.  But don't get in the way of a nesting mother; nesting is a biologically-driven need.

Choose less-toxic paints, which are cheaper and easier to redo than wallpaper, for the walls if you are redoing them.  Most baby furniture can be acquired secondhand, although you can expect that the eventual enforcement of CPSIA will make this a little more difficult (though perhaps cheaper, because more people will be willing to unload items on you for free).  See the rest of this chapter for my opinions on the various baby stuffs.

Most nursery furniture, if you decide to buy, can be purchased more cheaply by buying equivalent regular furniture.  Afford-

---

**Plagiocephaly**

Positional plagiocephaly is the flat spot on the back of the baby's head (and corresponding deformations on the other side) that occur when the back of the baby's head spends too much time against a hard surface.  Its incidence has increased in recent years, because of the "Back to Sleep" anti-SIDS campaign, because crib mattresses are very firm to avoid suffocation, and because modern babies have been spending a lot of time in car seats, buckets, bouncers, and swings, and on hard floors.

Treatment of plagiocephaly starts with correcting the positional problems.  In severe cases, a special helmet may be prescribed.

Prevent plagiocephaly (and save money!) by varying baby's lying positions, and by providing softer surfaces for them (while still avoiding suffocation hazards).  Also, minimize the amount of time that they spend in car seats and other seats.

---

124 See **http://www.carbuyingtips.com/** when you are ready to buy a car.

able solid wood pieces can be found at antique stores, but avoid painted items, because they may have lead paint.

## Car seat

Buying used car seats is not encouraged these days; they may have been recalled, or damaged in an accident, or simply be past their expiration date (most seats expire after five or six years[125]). The Consumer Product Safety Commission has a checklist[126] for determining whether a used car seat is safe to use. Basically, if you know the history of the seat and know that it has not been in any accidents, if the seat has not yet expired and has not been recalled, if all the parts are undamaged and in working order, and you have the seat manual to tell you how to install it properly, it should be safe.

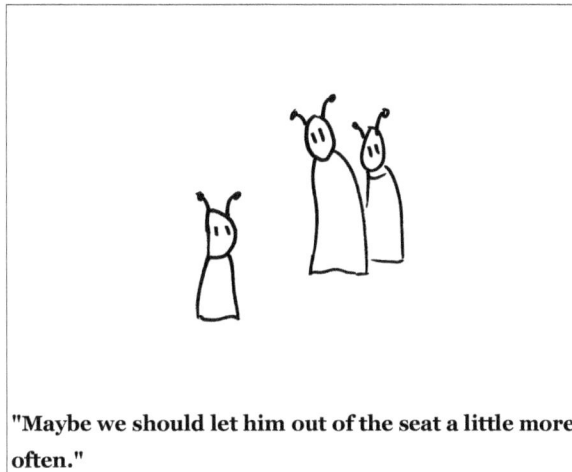

**"Maybe we should let him out of the seat a little more often."**

Convertible seats are a more frugal choice than bucket-style seats because they take much longer to outgrow. (But they may expire before they are outgrown, frustratingly, especially if they have spent months sitting on the store shelf before they are purchased.) The convertible seats are also much safer in an accident. The buckets are very difficult to carry around (they weigh as much as a newborn baby themselves, but the weight is more

---

125 Partly to keep parents buying the newest seats with the most recent safety innovations. In the 90's, so I've read, manufacturers would say that the seats were good for "about ten years".
126 Used child safety seat checklist: **http://www.cpsafety.com/articles/UsedSeat.aspx**

awkwardly distributed), and their use tends to lead to dangerous practices such as perching them, with baby inside, on shopping carts. The rise in the incidence of plagiocephaly (see sidebar) is largely from babies spending too much time in their buckets. Buckets are car seats, and come with a minimum of padding—to keep the straps working effectively in a car crash, when the padding is greatly compressed by the forces on the baby. So buckets are not really meant to be used as portable bassinets. There have also been problems with buckets not being correctly snapped into their car seat bases, or into strollers. The baby is not safe in a tumbling bucket! Finally, people seem to interact less with a baby that is strapped into a bucket, which doesn't help the baby's development any. Be smart, and minimize your baby's car seat time. Let them have some in-arms time and some baby carrier time.

*Baby Bargains* recommends getting an infant seat for the first few months, and then switching to a convertible, even though the infant seat may be outgrown by six months.

Five-point harnesses, and keeping your baby rear-facing as long as the seat will allow, are safest. Keep projectiles, such as toys and mirrors and other loose objects, to a minimum (for your own sake as well).

A car seat cover (that covers both seat and baby), or a spare wool blanket, or a home-made poncho, may be useful if you live somewhere with cold winters. Snowsuits and padded winter jackets are too bulky, and interfere with the protection afforded by car seats—protection that babies especially need when riding on slippery winter roads. On the other hand, hypothermia and frostbite are definite winter hazards as well. It is possible to unzip a winter coat, run the car seat straps under it and buckle them, and then zip the coat up over the harness.

## Complete travel system

It's a car seat! And a stroller! And a bucket that you can just lug around! I don't have much to say about this, except that it looks like something expensive that the baby will outgrow in a hurry. *Baby Bargains* says that they are heavy, and prone to break. It's possible to buy just a stroller frame, that will fit and support an infant car seat.

## *Stroller*

Sooner or later you will probably want one or two of these, although I do see a lot of empty strollers being pushed around, while the baby is being carried by a parent. (See the Baby Carriers section below for ways to save your arms.) Find a stroller that is sturdy, comfortable to push (check the handle height to make sure that it works for Dad as well as Mom), and folds up conveniently.

The big disadvantage of strollers is that they tend to restrict you to the paved sidewalks and trails. The public transit system in my area requires that strollers be folded up before boarding a bus. Strollers are also difficult to store in an apartment.

Babies need to be able to hold up their heads very well before they can ride in a jogging stroller, or even in a light umbrella stroller.

## *Baby carriers*

Babies love to be carried, but they weigh several pounds at birth, and only get heavier after that. Baby carriers help the baby to stay close to a warm, moving body, to see more of what is going on, and to be interacted with more. When they are ready to sleep, they can ease off to sleep.

There are a good many tutorials on "babywearing" and the different kinds of carriers online at The Mamatoto Project[127] and at thebabywearer.com.[128]

Baby carriers make it easier to go places where it is difficult to push or maneuver a stroller—hiking trails, for example. They also make it possible to go to the bathroom without putting the baby down.

### Slings

A sling is one very convenient way to carry a baby. When the baby is lying in the sling, it gives them a sense of enclosure and closeness to mom—like being back in the womb. Slings come in a variety of types, but basically all they are is a loop of strong cloth that goes over one shoulder, and the baby rides in the bottom of the loop. Some are adjust-

---

127 The Mamatoto Project is online at **http://www.wearyourbaby.com/**
128 The Babywearer site: **http://thebabywearer.com/**

able, some are not. Some have padding at the edges and the shoulder. Ideally, when you try on a sling, the bottom of the loop should hit your thigh when you stoop—you don't want the baby to ride too low on you.

Slings can cost anywhere from $25 on up. It is fairly easy (and much cheaper) to make your own, but you need to be careful to make it strong enough—choose sturdy fabric that has a little give to it. Heavily reinforce the edges and the seams—*very* heavily. If the seam starts to rip, you need time to catch the baby before they fall. If you make a ring sling, use heavy-duty rings that can take the weight.

Slings have a bit of a learning curve when you start, but not too bad of one. To put a baby in a sling, the best way is to put the sling on, and then put the baby in. Make sure that the baby isn't too scrunched, and has room to breathe. Also, make sure the sling material is spread out enough over your shoulder and back, otherwise it will start to cut your shoulder after a few minutes, in a very annoying way. So adjust it before the baby goes to sleep!

Padding at the shoulder and the rails is more useful for when your baby is older and heavier. If you keep an arm around them, they can sit upright on the sling, facing you, with their legs hanging down. You do have to watch for when they start to slip down through it, though.

The weakness of slings is that the weight of the baby is concentrated on one shoulder, and can throw the rest of your body out of whack if you are not careful. Switching sides now and then will help. For extended babywearing, a carrier that spreads the weight over both shoulders is better.

### Wraps and other baby carriers

A wrap is a long piece of cloth that is tied around the carrying person to make a custom-sized baby carrier. There are a variety of ways to tie a wrap,[129] but I have only learned one. It is very comfortable, and works well for long walks and extended babywearing, like a day at the State Fair, or a day hike.

---

129 See **http://www.wearyourbaby.com/** to learn more about different ways of tying a wrap, and all about baby carriers in general.

My wrap is five yards long, and 20 inches wide, made of a single piece of polar fleece; I followed Mamatoto's Make a Wrap instructions.  I bought five yards of 60-inch-wide fleece on sale; so I was able to make three wraps.  (Five yards is long enough to fit an XL size person.)  This is the tie that I learned (which they call the "Front (Proper) Cross Tie On First"; under Front Wrap Cross), practice on a stuffed animal or a small pillow before you try this on a real baby:

1.  Find the center of the wrap.

2.  Put the center at the small of your back.

3.  Bring both ends forward.

4.  Cross in front, throwing one end over each shoulder.

5.  Cross in back, and bring the ends forward again, around your waist.

6.  Tie in front at your waist.  If you have too much length left, run the ends around your waist another time, and tie them.

7.  The wrap should now make an "X" on the front of you, and another "X" on the back of you.  The baby goes in the front X, facing you.  (Not the back X, because they could fall out!  There are different tying methods for back carries.) See the back view below.  The front view is the same, except for the ends of the wrap hanging down where they are tied at the waist.

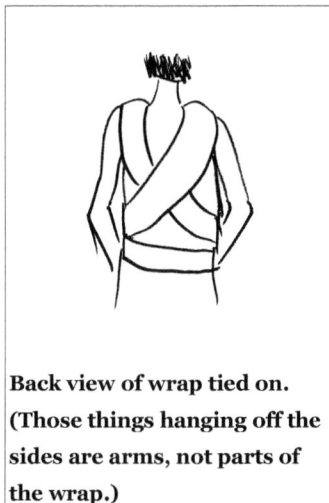

**Back view of wrap tied on. (Those things hanging off the sides are arms, not parts of the wrap.)**

8.  Lift up the baby.  Put the baby's first leg in so that it comes out the side of the X (not the bottom!).  Put the baby's second leg in so it comes out the other side of the X.  Now lower the baby in and spread each band over the baby's butt.

9.  Do a final check to make sure that the baby is well supported and won't fall out.

Be careful to support the baby when you lean forward, because the bands could part and the baby could fall right out.  Also be careful if the baby's head is tucked under the band: they could suddenly slip to the side and take a dive.

A mei tai/podeagi/Asian Baby Carrier is a square of cloth with four straps.  The square supports the baby and the straps attach it to the adult.  I would like to make one sometime, but I have never used one myself.

There are also more structured baby carriers available commercially, with straps and buckles and all that.  It is best if you can try before you buy.  Make sure that the baby's weight is supported at their legs, and not just at their crotch, and that the carrier distributes the weight over you well.  There can be quite a learning curve with these, too, in figuring out all the straps and buckles and clips.

There are also backpack-type carriers.  The best ones are made by real backpack makers, according to *Baby Bargains*, which I can well believe.

Babywearing is another skill that is best learned from a mentor.  If you see someone carrying a baby in a way that you want to learn, ask them to show you how!

## Crib

The essential characteristics of a crib are that it is an enclosed baby bed that little babies can't roll out of, and that bigger babies can't climb out of.  Mattresses are usually sold separately.

For sake of safety, check the sturdiness and bar spacing[130] before buying or accepting a crib—even on a new crib.[131]  Check how to raise and lower the sides, and if you will be able to do this quietly while holding a baby.  Make sure nothing is broken or missing.

130 Bar spacing should be less than 2 3/8 inches (or the diameter of a pop can).
131 As of this writing (September 2009), there have already been a half-dozen crib recalls this year.

Especially make sure that the mattress fits well, so the baby can't get stuck between the mattress and the crib (or anywhere else in it—there shouldn't be any cutouts in the headboard or footboard), and if it is painted, test for lead paint—older babies will chew on the rails. If you have pets, figure out how you are going to keep them out of the crib. Old cribs cause a significant proportion of the annual injuries and deaths of children, according to the Consumer Product Safety Commission.

The Consumer Product Safety Commission recently announced a ban on the manufacture, sale, and resale of drop-side cribs, beginning in June 2011. Hotels, motels, and daycares also are required to replace their drop-side cribs, by December 2012.

According to *Baby Bargains*, most cribs have to be ordered. Usually from China. They wait until a certain number of orders for that model of crib come in, and then they make a batch and ship them.[132] So if you are going to order a crib, order early.

Crib bumpers may keep a scooting baby from bumping into the bars, but they are also a hazard for the baby to get tangled in and trapped, or suffocated against. Older babies try to use them as steps to climb out of the crib.

Sleep positioners have also been implicated in some suffocation cases.

### Consider co-sleeping

The Bible says that Baby Jesus was wrapped in swaddling cloths and laid in a manger to sleep.[133] But remember that he was born in a stable, and the manger was probably the cleanest spot they could find for him. Also, with all the visitors to Bethlehem at the time, the stable was probably full, wall-to-wall, with donkeys belonging to the other visitors to Bethlehem—I picture one lone donkey standing outside, to make room for Mary to go in and give birth. There probably was a great danger of Baby Jesus being trampled if he co-

---

132 A process remarkably similar to the bridal gown production process exposed by the same authors (Denise and Alan Fields) in *Bridal Bargains*.

133 Luke Chapter 2, verses 12 and 16.

slept in the stable.[134] So I don't think the Nativity story can be used as Biblical evidence that God meant for babies to sleep in cribs.

While it is true that sleeping apart may lead to deeper, "better" sleep, most people seem to sleep "happier" near loved ones. My babies have been very content to have me within arm's reach all night. I have been happy to have them close, and very happy to almost never have to get out of bed (or fully wake up, even) for nighttime feedings. There is a synergy between co-sleeping and breastfeeding; they naturally go together.

Perhaps "The Couple's Realm" pattern in *A Pattern Language* needs to be augmented with "The Family Bed" and "The Family Realm" patterns. Little children do not respect "The Couple's Realm" without being trained to do so.

We have gotten by without using a crib at all, because we co-sleep on mattresses on the floor. We have never really had space for a crib, and if we had one, we would have had a hard time keeping the cat out of it. Our first child would never permit being put down to sleep, anyway. She woke up every time. Nor was there any hope of her going to sleep on her own, not until she had outgrown cribs entirely.

Conditioning a baby to sleep alone in a very dark, very quiet room can backfire on you later. The baby that learns to sleep on the go has an advantage during the times when the routine is disrupted. When I was in college, I had a horrible time trying to sleep while my roommates stayed up late to study.

Sometimes co-sleeping is linked to SIDS deaths. Actually, most of these co-sleeping deaths were from the baby getting suffocated by being squashed or trapped. Responsible co-sleeping is reasonably safe, and it would be more scientifically honest to separate the obvious suffocation deaths from the rest. The real SIDS rate for co-sleeping babies is probably lower, because hearing mom breathing nearby helps little babies keep their own breathing on track. Anyway, co-sleeping babies are much more likely to be breast-fed babies, and the benefits of breastfeeding far outweigh the risks of co-sleeping, as long as some simple safety guidelines are followed:

- Adults not incapacitated by alcohol, drugs, medications, or excessive fatigue.

---

134 Luke 11 and 1 Kings 3 contain other mentions of co-sleeping in Biblical times. The latter tells of a newborn's death by overlaying—possibly because the mother was overtired from giving birth without assistance.

- Baby co-sleeps next to mom (who tends to sleep lightly and be more aware of the baby), and away from dad and siblings and pets.

- Co-sleep on a bed or mattress, with a firm surface, not on a couch (to avoid suffocation and entrapment).

- No fall hazards off the side (I kept an arm around my baby if there was, and didn't leave them alone).  By the time the baby is rolling and scooting, it's best to put the mattress on the floor (with rugs or mats at the sides, if need be).

- Don't let baby fall into a crack between the mattress and the wall.

- Keep blankets and pillows away from baby.  Dress the baby in a sleep sack if it's cold.

- Don't let baby overheat; mom provides a lot of heat.

- Childproof the room very, very carefully if you are going to let them sleep alone at all.

The best part about co-sleeping is that the mother and baby's sleep cycles can synchronize, so the baby's feedings don't disrupt mom's cycles of deeper sleep.  For breastfeeding, mom can wake up just enough to help the baby latch on, and then both can drift easily back to sleep.  This is how I managed to do night feedings for months (and years) at a time, without getting too sleep-deprived.  (Also, I slept in and took naps whenever I could.)

The second best thing about co-sleeping is being able to see your child, who probably did not manage to be a little angel *all* day long, turn back into one at night.

Co-sleeping, paradoxically, can lead to a larger family, perhaps because people who are willing to share their bed with their babies are more open to letting their lives be further changed by additional babies.  (And also more creative in finding opportunities for intimacy with small children around.)  Co-sleeping is much easier on both parents and children, and so additional babies are "cheaper" in terms of effort.

So, instead of buying a crib, consider buying yourself a good (and large) mattress.  You will need it.  The bed frame is optional.

But in the end, what matters most is that everyone gets a good night's sleep, one way or another.

## *Bassinet*

A bassinet may be handy, if you want the baby to sleep near you for a few months, but not in your bed. But it is very quickly outgrown, when the baby starts being able to roll and scoot out of it, so really a clothes basket or a dresser drawer, set on the floor and lined with a blanket (safely), would be just as good. We had a bassinet, for a while, but the cat immediately claimed it as a kitty bed.

## *Changing table*

It is perfectly possibly to live without a changing table, but we do use ours—changing diapers on the floor is too hard on my back. It is also nice to have a washable surface for changing really messy diapers on, and a place to keep all the cloth diapers and diaper covers. It does take up a lot of room, and is not terribly sturdy. If we hadn't had one handed down to us, I would prefer a small dresser with a changing pad on top, which would be useful well past the diaper years.

Whatever changing surface you use, pay attention to the ergonomics—you will be changing thousands of diapers over the years. The better the changing area is set up, the faster, easier, and more pleasant changing diapers will be.

Ideally, our bathroom would be big enough to accommodate a changing table, but it is not. We put the changing table as close to the bathroom as possible, for wetting wipes and for washing hands afterward. Take good care to keep your baby from falling off the changing table, you never know when they're going to roll over for the very first time.

## *Rocker and footstool and chair*

This may be a good item to splurge on. For holding the baby, and for breastfeeding, it should have arms at a comfortable height, and should have some sort of footstool.

For nursing at the computer, I have a chair that can swivel and tilt back, with arms, and a do-it-myself footstool. I also switch the mouse back and forth, depending on which hand I have free at the moment.

## *Playpen or play yard*

Play yard is the current name for these, but I still think of them as playpens.

I was given a playpen for my first child, and almost never used it. When she was a little baby, it was pointless to confine her in it, because she couldn't go anywhere. When she started crawling, she hated the playpen because she wanted room to scoot around. Same thing with pulling up and walking. By the time she could walk, she could climb out of the playpen and fall out of it. I only pulled it out when she was two and had a little brother, and was starting to need a little space of her own, before we could give her her own bedroom.

So I think standard-size playpens are only useful in certain circumstances, like if you want to keep the baby from getting trampled by the dog, if you're staying somewhere that's impossible to childproof, or if you need to confine a pre-climber for a few minutes so you can take a shower. Larger play yards may be useful for keeping the baby confined, but not *too* confined.

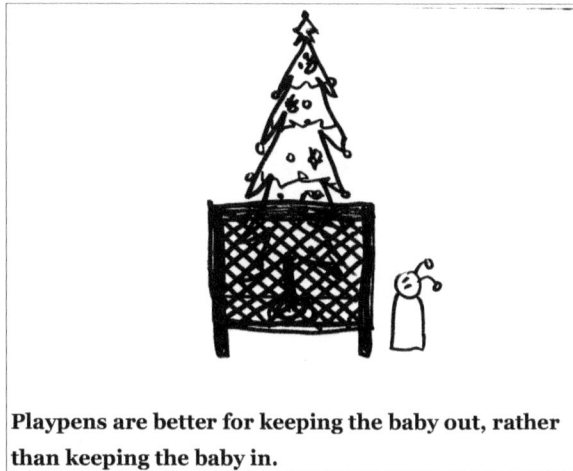

**Playpens are better for keeping the baby out, rather than keeping the baby in.**

Old playpens probably don't meet modern safety standards. Many were recalled for collapsing on babies.

## Swings and bouncers and gyms and activity centers

These are the kind of things that you might as well wait and see on until you know for sure that your baby will like them. I think they are most useful for the few months when the baby can use their hands to grasp toys, but can't yet sit up by themselves. They do take up a lot of room. Some mothers use them as baby containers, while they take a shower.

## Baby bathtub

Little babies don't go out and roll in the mud, so they don't really need baths that often, until they start crawling and experimenting with solid food. But by that time they will be trying to climb out of any baby-sized bathtub. So far I have bathed my babies only in the bathroom sink, the kitchen sink, and the bathtub (by having them take a bath with me). The current baby prefers the bathtub; he feels safe with me right there holding him, and he loves to splash. A baby bathtub will also take up a lot of space when you're not using it.

Turning your water heater down to 120° F, if you can, is much safer for you and the baby, and can save money as well. Still, you should always check the water temperature on yourself, before putting the baby in.

## Bedding

Simple flannel receiving blankets are great: for swaddling, peekaboo, emergency flat diapers, and burp rags.

Quilts are considered unsafe for baby bedding these days, but they make good rolling-around-on pads for the floor—for a few months, until the baby achieves mobility. We also let our toddler sleep on a baby quilt when she's sick—it is easier to wash and replace than a king-size sheet. (This is how we get away with having only two spare sheets while co-sleeping.)

If you're using a crib, get a good half-dozen crib sheets.

## *Clothing*

Babies outgrow clothes very quickly—about every three months in the beginning. People love to give baby clothes as gifts. To keep track of all those little outfits, the best thing to do is make a master list of clothing needed, organized by size, and then check off what comes in. Then you can easily see what you have too much of, and what you still need to buy.

If you are planning on having more children later, and want more gender-neutral baby clothes, keep the baby's sex a secret until the baby is born. I also keep "Will this work for both boys and girls?" in mind when I am shopping for baby clothes. The more the boy/girl wardrobes can overlap, the less space you will need to store them. Also, check *Baby Bargains* for the best baby clothing brands, so you know which ones are likely to last long enough for several children.

The main difficulty with baby clothes is that infants grow about one size per season. (Except that some grow faster, and some grow more slowly.) Figuring out what size your baby is likely to be in each season will help you select baby clothing. Remember that you can layer clothing on the baby in the cooler months. Babies that are learning to stand and walk will do better in outfits that leave their feet bare.

You may also receive a friend's stash of baby clothes. This can be daunting to sort through, as I discovered when I was bestowed with the accumulated outgrown clothes of the last *three* babies at my church.

Finally, the best place to buy baby clothes is yard sales—find the right sale, and you can pick up a lot of baby clothing for only a few dollars. The CPSIA law has led some thrift stores to stop selling children's clothing entirely; if the Consumer Product Safety Commission ever really starts enforcing this law, it may become much more difficult to find used baby clothes.

Babies can get away without shoes, for most occasions, until they are close to being able to walk. Both of mine have had quite a talent for kicking off booties—we have carried them barefoot into many places. For the walking baby, some people now recommend only shoes with very thin, flexible soles, so that the baby's foot can bend when they walk.

Look for a person or place that you can give excess baby clothes to, to keep the quantity down to a manageable level. Inevitably, some baby clothes will become threadbare favorites, while others are hardly ever worn at all.

When looking for baby clothes, consider these things:

- Make sure that there is nothing scratchy on the inside of the clothing.

- For shirts and one-piece suits, can it easily go over baby's head? Arms?

- Is there easy access to the diaper for diaper changes?

- If you are going to use cloth diapers, is there enough room for the extra bulk?

- What fibers is it made of? Cotton is comfortable and can take hard washing. Wool is warm, but needs special care.

## Toys

The best toys are the simple old classics. A few favorites: wood blocks, plastic cups that stack and nest, stacking rings, toys that rattle and jingle.

Teething toys: Babies will put any toy into their mouths to explore its taste and texture, but it is important to have toys that are good for teething. Teething is a painful and slow process, and gnawing on toys helps babies to cope.

> **The One Million Times Rule**
>
> The baby's possessions should all be things that the parents are willing to read, pick up, put away, scrub, watch, play with, or listen to One Million Times.

Avoid toys that are over-engineered, over-stylized, and over-priced. Weed out toys that you yourself don't like—apply the One Million Times Rule—and only allow toys that you won't mind picking up one million times. Be frugal and refuse to replace the batteries of any toy that makes annoying electronic noises.

Making a firm rule that only blood relatives are allowed to give your child stuffed animals would also be wise. (Wise, but impossible to enforce.)

**Choking, Strangulation, and Poisoning Hazards**

Avoid toys that can fit entirely within the baby's mouth; anything less than 1 ¼ inches by 2 ¼ inches or so. Watch out for toys with small parts that could come loose. Avoid toys with cords longer than seven inches. Avoid toys that might contain lead paint and toys with metal parts that might contain lead in their alloys. Try to keep electrical cords out of baby's reach, too.

Some people try to encourage the baby to bond with a "lovey", a toy that the baby can drag around for comfort. My preference has been to not attempt to replace personal attention and love from me with toys. This is more work at first, but saves trouble later on, as the mis-placement (or even the laundering) of a lovey toy can be very upsetting to a baby. Some parents buy duplicate loveys, and switch them occasionally.

For the rest, let babies play with real things as much as possible: metal pots and pans and wooden spoons, for exam-ple. The whole world is novel and incred-ibly exciting to them. They are busily constructing their entire mental model of reality. Take the baby outside and supervise as they explore rocks, grass, sand, dirt, flowers, twigs, leaves, caterpillars, bugs, mud, puddles, weeds, seeds, nuts. The more that they can engage with the real world and learn about it, the better. (But don't let them eat sand by the handful, or choke on acorns, or grab a fistful of nettles, or things like that, of course.)

## Educational stuff

There are lots of toys and videos and other products promising to make your baby a high-achieving genius. The truth is, that the best way to educate your baby and help them reach their full potential is to interact with them and let them watch as you go about your business. Balance that with time for them to practice their developing skills on their own, and there you have it. No need to buy anything.

The American Association of Pediatrics recommends no television until at least the age of two.

Instead of TV, sing them songs while you're working, and hone your vocal skills, while also passing on your cultural heritage. Install "a lovely bookshelf on your wall"[135] (anchor it to the wall so they can't pull it over onto themselves) and read, read, read to them.

## Diaper bag

One helpful hint I once heard was to use a camera bag as a diaper bag, and a diaper bag as a camera bag. I am not a big fan of cutesy diaper bags. Our favorite diaper bag is constructed as a small backpack, with a built-in changing pad.

The diaper bag doesn't need to be very large. All you need are diapers, wipes, maybe a changing pad, possibly sunscreen, definitely a change of clothes for the child. We also put toys and snacks into the bag, for convenient hauling.

Don't stock too many diapers in the diaper bag when the baby is growing fast—too many will be outgrown before you get around to using them.

## Health, safety, and sanity items (alphabetized)

These are the things that we have found most (or least) useful to have on hand:

**Acetaminophen/ibuprofen:** Have some in case of fever. Get a dosage chart (dosages based on baby's age and size) from your doctor ahead of time.

**Allergy stuff (Benadryl® and the like):** Have some ready for your baby's first encounter with a bee.

**Baby monitor:** Whether or not this would be useful for you depends on the layout of your home. In a small home, it is probably not needed. In a larger home, it may be useful. In any case, they use the same radio frequencies as some other consumer electronics, so be careful to keep your private business off the air, and don't be surprised if devices interfere with each other.

**Baby shampoo and body wash:** How much you will need depends on how often you plan to bathe your baby. Little babies tend to not get very dirty, except for their necks. Liquid baby soaps are also good for washing your hands after diaper changes;

---

135 As recommended by Roald Dahl in *Charlie and the Chocolate Factory*.

they don't dry out your skin too much. This matters when you are changing eight or ten or twelve diapers a day.

**Childproofing items:** baby gates, outlet covers, cabinet locks, toilet latches, refrigerator locks, padding for hard corners,[136] wall straps and anchors for bookcases; the list goes on and on. Most of these your child will learn to thwart, sooner or later, depending on their temperament. Childproof first for the hazards that are most likely to be fatal: falls, drowning, poisoning, electrocution, cuts.[137] You will not be able to prevent every bump and bruise, and it is a good thing for babies to learn from experience to be careful for themselves. Remember, they are forming their whole conception of reality, from scratch. They need to put "If I bang into something that is hard, it will hurt" into their personal knowledge base,[138] and to develop a reasonable sense of self-preservation. Also, childproofing props and gadgets cannot replace proper adult supervision.

It is worth doing a good crawl-through of your home, before the baby gets mobile. Things look a lot different from a baby's perspective; electrical cords and outlets are especially intruiging.

For the things that really do need locking up, install real metal locks. Your baby is going to grow into an active toddler, and then into an inquisitive and resourceful pre-schooler.

I am going to put slipcovers in the childproofing category—do your future self a big favor and make or buy good cotton slipcovers for all of your upholstered furniture. Alexandra Stoddard, the interior decorator, highly recommends them,[139] because cotton can take hard laundering, while most upholstery is very, very difficult to clean.

**CPR class:** If you haven't learned infant and child CPR, or need a refresher course, it is easiest to take a class before the baby is born. You should also learn how to do the versions of the Heimlich maneuver that are appropriate for babies and toddlers.

---

136 *Baby Bargains* tells of parents who use foam pipe wrapping for corner padding.

137 Outlet covers are much more effective than outlet plugs, which can be a choking hazard once the baby figures out how to pull them out.

138 In artificial intelligence, a "knowledge base" is a collection of facts that the artificial intelligence has been told, or has learned or inferred for itself.

139 In *The Decoration of Houses,* page 361.

**Earplugs (for you):** Absolutely essential. While you should always try to comfort your child, not all hurts can be charmed away with a kiss. Babies always have a reason for crying, but you won't always be able to figure out what it is. Sometimes, it seems like they just need to have a Good, Long Fuss. Earplugs can save your sanity while you are trying to help your child cope with their pains and frustrations.

**Earplugs (for the baby):** We have given the kind that fits in the outer ear a try. They are helpful, but do not provide good enough ear protection to get the baby through an action movie in the theater.

**Diaper rash cream:** The zinc oxide kind is useful, sometimes. A frugal option is to leave the baby's bottom bare for a while, and let fresh air and sunshine do the work. (Keep creams away from cloth diapers by using a diaper liner, they are difficult to wash out.)

**Hand sanitizer:** This will be useful to you to have, mostly for use after diaper changes on the go, but it's not all that helpful at keeping kids from getting sick, in my opinion—before you can get to them with the hand sanitizer, they have already put their grubby fingers in their mouths, and eyes, and noses.

**Humidifier:** I have no opinion on this, except to try to find one that doesn't leak all over the hardwood floor (as our first one did), and that is easy to clean. (It doesn't do your baby any good to have the humidifier spray moldy water into the air.)

**Lead paint tests:** There may be lead paint lurking in some odd place within your home, or lead in other forms. Cast iron tubs with their enamel coating chipped is one source of lead that surprises many people.

**Nail clippers:** One of the worst moments in breastfeeding is when the baby hooks a sharp little claw into some very tender Mom skin. Clipping a baby's nails is a perilous job: it is too easy to nick them and draw blood with baby nail clippers. So I use a pair of sharp (but blunt-tipped) scissors instead—it makes nail trimming faster, easier, *and* safer—less risk of nicking the baby.

**Nipple ointment (for Mom):** May be helpful in the early days of breastfeeding. After that, nipples generally want to be left alone when not on feeding duty. If it is lanolin, the ointment can be used to lanolinize wool diaper covers.

**Ponytail holders or hair clips (for Mom):** To keep long hair up and away from grabby baby hands.

**Shopping cart cover:** Shopping carts are teeming with obnoxious germs. (You probably shouldn't touch them with your own bare hands!) It is possible to buy a shopping cart cover that covers every part of the cart that the baby might touch, and keeps them buckled in to boot, but a simpler solution is to carry the baby in a baby carrier while you shop.

**Sunscreen:** Perhaps helpful, but we only use it to prevent sunburn, not to prevent sun exposure. Recent research has revealed myriad benefits to getting sufficient vitamin D, and a number of health risks from not getting enough. And who knows whether the chemicals in sunscreen are really safe, or not.

**Teething medicine:** Helpful. Babies spend a lot of their first year teething. Try a little on your own gums to see how strong it is.

**Toothbrush and toothpaste:** It is nice to have special baby toothbrushes and toothpaste, but not absolutely necessary. You can clean the baby's teeth with a clean washcloth.

**Thermometer:** Nice to have, but you can tell nearly as much about the severity of a fever by feeling the child's forehead, and by observing their behavior to see if they are acting like they are sick.

## Pacifiers

Pacifiers are a substitute for suckling at the breast. Some babies have a high need to suck. Other times, babies want to suck for comfort, but Mom is unavailable or out of reach—such as when riding in a car. For breastfeeding babies, it is recommended to avoid pacifiers for the first six weeks, to get nursing well established.

The downside of giving the baby a pacifier is that then the baby knows that pacifiers exist. You gain some freedom from having to comfort nurse the baby, but then you become the Pacifier Retriever. And you will not be able to see the baby's smiles nearly as well. (My unscientific observation is that people talk and interact much less with babies sucking on pacifiers.) Later on, you will have to wean the baby from the pacifier.

Instead of a pacifier, you can let the baby suck on the end of your little finger, or comfort nurse at the breast.

## Books and magazines to tell you what to do

There are plenty of parenting books out there. The best ones are the ones that support your God-given parenting instincts and your authority as a parent. Watch out for, and avoid, books written by men to teach women how to mother. The Bible says that it is the job of *older women in the church* to teach the younger women how to mother.[140] As an online article by Helen Aardsma put it[141]:

> The simple question is: What do men really *know* about the womanly arts anyway?

Men who try to take on this role have a strong tendency to deride maternal instincts and try to override them with "rational and scientific" approaches. Bad idea. I have noticed that the few exceptions to this, the books written by men that support maternal instincts and natural mothering, are different for one very good reason: the men are writing about *what they have learned from women.*

Sadly, most of the older women who should be teaching the younger women, were taken in by the male parenting authorities of their own time. Much has been lost, as Mrs. Aardsma says in her article.

Susan Strasser, in *Never Done: A History of American Housework*,[142] points out that the advent of the scientific baby experts came at the end of the nineteenth century, and the beginning of the twentieth century, and that the experts had some self-interest in dismissing maternal instincts:

> If mother love sufficed, if maternal instinct knew best, there was no place for the experts or the books they wrote.

---

140 In the New Testament book of Titus, Chapter 2.

141 Online article "Woman to Woman" at

**http://www.themotherscompanion.org/newsletters/womantowomansample.php**

142 Page 234.

I do think that mothering is in part a learned behavior. Books by traditional mothers are better than nothing, but a poor replacement for having a real, live mentor.

Another thing to watch out for in books—undermining parental authority—you can see in many books written by self-proclaimed experts (such as nannies), who think they need to educate idiot parents. While I may be an idiot parent, I have spent thousands of hours with my children, and I am the reigning expert on each particular child now. Likewise, you will become the reigning expert on your own baby. Parenting and babysitting are not the same thing.

Some people, like me, who have one or two cute-smart-well-behaved-healthy children, think that they know it all, and want to pass it on to you. They believe all sorts of silly things that a third, or fourth, or fifth child might cure them of thinking. Be smart and look for people with large families, whose children have a variety of temperaments.

There is no such thing as a perfect baby, and no such thing as a perfect parent, and no one should promise to make either you or your baby perfect. Nor is there a perfect one-size fits all routine that works for everyone. You have to take from all advice the things that will work for you in your situation, and just leave the rest.

I would also say to not have too many parenting books or experts around—too many confusing differences of opinion. One or two good ones is plenty.

Magazines are entertaining to read, but most of the articles are thinly-veiled advertisements sandwiched between even more advertisements. They can't tell you "You don't really need to buy all this crap," because that would offend their advertisers. So caring for a baby naturally, easily, and frugally tends to be disparaged. The typical magazine article is even more poorly researched than this book, and many factual errors make it through the editorial process. They also present an overly idealized picture of parenthood and babyhood, which can make you very dissatisfied on the days when both parents and baby are fussy.

## *Recording gear*

Everyone wants to record those special baby moments: first smile, first step, first fall. But your cameras could easily cost more than your baby did. Here are my opinions on the subject, colored by my experience of having an amateur photographer for a husband.

Hiring a professional photographer would be a major splurge. So is going to a photo studio, although sometimes they have specials.

If you don't want to get a camera, or, like me, find that the camera batteries are dead every time you want to take a picture, maybe a baby book or baby journal would work better—write a note of the cute thing the baby was doing, rather than take a picture.

I cannot give you any advice on scrapbooking, other than that I have heard many mothers complain that they don't have enough time to scrapbook every event that they would like to. And that I see, from visiting the scrapbooking store, that it is a hobby that you could easily spend a lot of money on.

A new camera might be a good splurge. You don't absolutely need to have a computer to have a digital camera, unless you want to do photo editing or backups—you can take the camera's memory card in to offload the pictures that you want printed. Film cameras are still around, though film as a medium seems to be waning—film manufacturers are dropping the less popular varieties of film. Digital pictures are easy to e-mail to family and friends, and post online.

But overall, film is the more stable medium for photographs. My old physics professor used to call black and white negatives "the closest thing we have to a time machine"—they can easily last 100 years if properly processed and stored. Digital data, on the other hand, tends to degrade more rapidly: files get misplaced, hard drives die, CDs wear out, technology moves on. As another physics professor of mine put it: "Fifty years ago, I could read this book. Fifty years from now, someone will still be able to read it. Can you say that for this data file? No!" (He remembers the days when data was stored on large reels of magnetic tape. And when they programmed with punch cards.)

So, for digital pictures, I recommend getting prints made of the ones that are most important to you, and (if you are storing pictures on your computer) backing up files to a separate hardware device. For film, store your negatives someplace safe. It is possible, although expensive, to have your negatives scanned and digital files created from them.

Developing black and white film yourself is not too hard to do at home, with a little equipment, chemicals, and time. My husband does this now and then, sometimes even using instant coffee and washing soda in the developing process.

For color film, and digital pictures, the other main option for getting prints is to take them somewhere that can print them for you. Or get your own photo printer; expect the printer to be cheap and the ink and photo paper to be expensive.

The new option that has developed in the last few years is to create your own photo-book: use your computer and your digital pictures to make a one-of-a-kind book, which you upload to the publisher, and order copies to be printed for you. This is actually an economical way of printing photos, but it takes a lot of time to lay out and put pictures into the book the way you want them. My husband the photographer has done several of these now, and they look very good. The price has been about $40 for a one-hundred-page softcover book with color pictures. One thing to watch out for is that the printing in the physical book is done well—sometimes there are printing flaws and you might need to have the publisher reprint it for you.

Anyway, if you are looking to buy a digital camera, don't worry too much about the number of megapixels that it has. Any new camera you can buy will have more than enough. A higher number of megapixels often means a higher number of "noise" pixels (i.e., little dots of static) in your pictures. Instead, worry about the responsiveness of the camera—how long does it take to take the picture, after you press the shutter button? Children are moving targets, in expression as well as in trajectory, and it is very frustrating to always have the camera take the picture half a second too late.

My husband's hint on organizing digital photographs is to make a folder each time you upload/unload pictures to your computer, and to name it like this: "yyyy-mm-dd--title". So if, say, on August 12, 2009 we went to the zoo and he took pictures, he would label the folder "2009-08-12--Zoo trip". Then, when he is digging through all his folders and folders of pictures (all stored together in one enormous folder), the alphabetization of the folder names will automatically put them into chronological order.

To take good photographs, pay attention to Focus, Composition, Timing/Luck, and Editing.  A good picture has to have something that is in focus, preferably the subject.  Composition is how the elements of the picture fit into the shape of the picture.  In some good pictures, you capture exactly the right moment just by luck.  Finally, with a good photo editing program and some editing skills, you can turn a mediocre picture into a good one.

My hint is to take some pictures of your child's favorite toys and books and playmates and pets for them, as well as some of the home, in case you move someday.  These are things the child will want to remember later.

With a digital camera, it is easy to take lots and lots and lots and lots of pictures.  My husband hates to delete *anything*—he may be able to make a good picture out of it later.  He also notes that a picture may take on special meaning later on, if a person in it dies prematurely.

I only take a small handful of pictures, and keep even less.  There are diminishing returns to taking pictures.  It is entirely possible to take so many that you won't have enough time later in life to even look at them all.

As for video recorders, I know very little about these, except, from sad experience, that they should not be dropped onto the hard surface of the parking lot.

## *Lifestyle changes*

For the sake of your own sanity, minimize workload, time commitments and obligations now, before the baby is born.  Get major time-consuming chores out of the way and done.  Wrap up loose ends and drop out of as many things as you can.  Don't worry, it's only temporary; a short season in your life.  One wise mother said that she just didn't plan on getting anything done in a year where she was having a baby.  Another said[143]:

> It wasn't until my husband and I had our third child that we finally realized that being parents **should** change our lives drastically and that we should curtail outside activities and direct our energies and efforts primarily on our family respon-

---

143 From the online article "Mommy Burnout" by Rebecca Prewett at
**http://www.fix.net/~rprewett/burnout.html** [Site unavailable, unfortunately—Dec. 2010]

sibilities during this season of our lives. The idea that we should "do it all" is a recipe for burnout and usually means that we end up doing none of it well.

With a baby, there is so much to do: feedings and diapers and baths and helping your baby cope with the frustrations of being little and immobile and inarticulate and teething. And things like lying under the trees watching the leaves move in the wind, and sitting in the yard exploring the exciting new textures of grass and sand. The baby will grow quickly, but while it does, you will have to go slowly.

## *Surviving the baby showers*

If you follow even half of the advice in this book, your baby shower registry will be very short. One hint in registering is not to register for specific baby clothes, beyond the very basics that are always in stock. Store clothing inventories change with the seasons, and will turn over significantly by the time that many people get around to shopping. If there is a must-have cute outfit in the store, buy it yourself before it's gone. Likewise, if you return some baby clothes after the shower, you may only get the clearance price credited back to you. Some people, in purchasing baby clothing for gifts, may fail to match the clothing size to the age that the baby will be when they need the clothing. (One couple that we know was stuck with buying their baby's entire wardrobe, because nothing that they were given fit the baby at the right time.)

When it is shower time, smile and be thankful for the generosity of others. Your baby is a blessing to them, as well as to you. Take careful note of who gave what, and send thank-you notes. Especially to the people who included a gift receipt.

## *Frugal baby announcements*

I have no particular hints for frugally and creatively announcing the birth of the baby, except that you should probably at least address the envelopes before the baby is born. (I didn't, and my second child is still unannounced, at six months of age.) For the first child, we used a photo printer and a labelmaker to print pictures and labels for baby announcements.

# *Final preparations for childbirth*

There's a lot to do in the last few weeks of waiting for the baby to arrive. Pack the suit-case (or, for a homebirth, buy the last few birth supplies and some food for the midwife), fill up the freezer with nutritious, easy-to-prepare meals, make a list of people to call with the news. Make sure there's plenty of gas in the car. Install the car seat. Have some newborn-sized diapers ready.

If you've made a birth plan, hopefully you've been able to go over it with your care-giver and have them sign off on it. I've heard that the best birth plans for hospital births are individualized, and short enough to fit on an index card. Long, checklist-like stand-ardized birth plans may get little respect.

If you're going to the hospital, plan on taking food with you. Lots of good food. Their ideas about when and what you need to eat are unlikely to coincide with yours (if they even remember to feed you at all, which may fail to happen, and guess how I know). Eating and drinking during a long labor can help keep a mother's strength going. The risk of throwing up is high, especially near transition, but the risk of having to go under general anesthesia and of aspirating vomit is low. After the hard work of giving birth, every mother deserves a good meal if she wants one, even if it's the middle of the night.

First babies often are born after their due date—mostly because the standard due date calculation doesn't allow for the fact that first pregnancies run about a week longer, on average, than later ones. Often women feel a great deal of pressure to induce, for no real reason besides the date circled on the calendar. You can ask for a Bishop's score, which looks at the state of the cervix and the position of the baby. The score is not at all predictive of when you will go into labor (this could happen either very soon, or not soon at all, regardless of your current state), but if it is low, then an induction is likely to fail.

# 7

# When the Baby Comes

Pregnancy is a long journey, but when it ends, you start on an even longer journey.

## *Meeting your child*

Birthing a baby is hard work, but there is a reward: meeting your baby! The sooner after the birth that you can hold them close, and the sooner that they take their first nursing, the better. Weighing and washing and all that hospital stuff can wait (although sadly it often doesn't).

Being born is hard work, too, and the baby will probably be nearly as tired and sore as you are. Rest together.

## *Signs that breastfeeding is going well*

It's difficult, in the early days, to know how well breastfeeding is going. The first couple days, only a little colostrum is produced, but just-born babies have tiny stomachs. Here are some things to look for:

- Baby is eating every two or three hours.
- Baby's lower lip is turned out while nursing, and baby is sucking on the areola, not just the nipple.

- You can hear the baby swallowing, and can see the muscles in front of and below the baby's ear working while they nurse.

- Baby passes meconium in the first day or so.

- After that, baby is regularly producing wet and poopy diapers.

- Mother's milk comes in, with feelings of engorgement, and of the milk "letting down" to flow to the baby, a couple of days after the birth. She starts to produce milk by the ounce.

Hopefully, breastfeeding will go well right from the start. But for many moms, especially the first time, it doesn't. Get help early, and often, preferably from someone who has a lot of training and experience in helping with breastfeeding problems: a lactation consultant, a La Leche League leader, or some other breastfeeding mentor. Don't be afraid to keep looking until you find the right person to help you with your particular problem. If you can get nursing going well within the first two weeks, you have a good chance of making it work. Even if it doesn't work out well by that time, you will probably be able to at least partially breastfeed. Remember, "you get better at the things that you do", and so does the baby. Even newborns can be fast learners.

Tongue tie, where the baby has extra tissue under or behind the tongue that prevents the full range of tongue motion needed for breastfeeding, is one problem that frequently goes unrecognized, even by lactation consultants. If you have a lot of nipple soreness, or the baby seems to be chomping more than sucking while feeding, or you notice that the baby can't stick his or her tongue out very far, then you should look into this.

## *Recovery*

For a fast and easy recovery, spend the first days resting well, and eating well. If there was ever a time that a woman deserved to be waited on hand and foot, this is it. Stay in bed with the baby, have a "babymoon", and let the other stuff go. Try not to run around the hospital, or back and forth to the doctor, unless you absolutely have to. Your job is to rest, recover, care for the baby, and bond.

Don't let the hospital put you in a panic about jaundice and kernicterus—jaundice is normal, more than half of all babies get some level of jaundice, and the baby's odds of dying of kernicterus (brain damage from excessively high bilirubin levels) are about one in a million. The best thing to do for jaundice is make sure that the baby is eating well; this helps the baby flush out the bilirubin.[144] Jaundice can make babies very sleepy; wake them up to feed them.

All mothers need a super-nutritious diet after giving birth. Mothers who are breast-feeding and mothers who have had caesareans especially need to eat well. Iron-rich foods are needed, and perhaps an iron supplement as well (though these may contribute to postpartum constipation).

Breastfeeding mothers need to start "eating for two"—roughly 500 extra calories a day. This translates into a only a few extra dollars a week in the food budget. Some-times "cow foods" like oatmeal and alfalfa are suggested, to help boost the milk supply. Occasionally foods in the mother's diet don't agree well with the baby: dairy products, or strongly-flavored foods like broccoli. Sometimes caffeine seems to cause problems. Watch for patterns of fussiness that are related to your eating.

Breastfeeding mothers are often told to keep taking their prenatal vitamins. After giving birth, I have switched to a chewable children's vitamin, because choking down huge prenatal vitamin pills is one of my least favorite parts of pregnancy.

Often, nursing mothers think that they aren't allowed to drink alcohol, but apparently drinking in small amounts is okay. (I don't drink, so I don't miss it, except on the days where my husband works late, and the baby is fussy, and the toddler is two years old, going on two.)

Let others meet your baby, slowly, and not all at once. Little babies need their rest, too.

## *Back to (house)work*

When you are up and around again, you can start getting the household under control again, one baby step at a time. Lower your expectations for now; just get the basics

---

144 The American Association of Pediatrics Practice Guidelines for newborn jaundice (also known as hyperbilirubinemia) can be found at **http://aappolicy.aappublications.org/cgi/content/ full/pediatrics%3B114/1/297**

done. Learning how to do them with a baby around is a whole new challenge. This is where the sling or other baby carrier is helpful—you can get things done, and the baby is happy being near you.

Keep track of the bills; the birth of a baby tends to throw budgets and bill-paying routines off track. Late payment fees are no fun, and not frugal.

The best time to cook dinner is during the baby's afternoon nap (if you are not napping yourself). At least get all the prep work done. Babies have a "witching hour" right around dinner time that makes it very difficult to accomplish anything, and then you are tempted to use expensive convenience foods or takeout.

## Paperwork

Typically, the hospital or other care provider takes care of the birth certificate and Social Security card paperwork. (If you are going to claim the child on your taxes, you will need to get a Social Security number for them.) You'll get the papers in the mail a few weeks later. It may cost a few dollars to order copies of the baby's birth certificate. I usually order two: one for us as parents, and one to give the child later on.

Also be sure to add the baby to your health insurance plan. The sooner, the better, so your insurance can start paying out benefits for the baby. Your insurance plan may have a deadline for this.

## Out and about

Little babies are portable. They can go lots of places where toddlers who run around and get into everything can't. Little babies are popular; the worlds of adults and children are so segregated nowadays that many adults go weeks without seeing a baby. Older people, especially, appreciate being able to touch a new little life. There is the whole world for your baby to learn about. Grab the diaper bag and go!

# *The new normal*

The family has to adjust to the new family member. The family's finances have to adjust as well. The mother has to adjust to the changes that pregnancy and birth and breast-feeding have wrought in her body.

Once the baby is a few months old, and things have settled down a little, try to take some time to check over your finances, and everything else, and see how things are going. You may need to make some adjustments in your budget, or some decisions about whether to work, or how much to work. No doubt there are still some aftershocks from the birth of the baby working themselves out. You will find new points of equilibrium (places where everything is in balance and at rest) for yourself and your family.

# 8

# The Growing Baby

The growing baby is a hard-working baby—laboriously developing one new skill after another. Here are some things that will come into play as your baby grows.

## *Starting solid food*

Around the age of six months or so, the baby will be getting teeth, and will be ready to start trying out solid food. Solid food is mainly for practice and fun, for the next few months. Even at one year, they may be taking in more than half of their nutrition from breastmilk or formula. (Hold off on cow's milk until a good, nutritious solid-food diet has been established.)

Baby food by the jar is incredibly expensive, but there are other options. One is to make your own baby food at home: peel it if necessary, cook it well, puree it, and store it. The easiest way to store it is to freeze it in baby-size portions—some people use an ice cube tray for this step—which can be thawed as needed.

Or you could just feed the baby a little of what you are eating; either with an inexpensive little food mill, or by what I call the "mooch and mash" method. For "mooch and mash", let the baby mooch little bits off your plate (except for things they could choke on). Mash up some of your food with a fork to feed to the baby (with a spoon). It is recommended to space out the introduction of new foods to the baby, so you will know what food caused an allergic reaction, if they have one.

The food mill is a little hand grinder that purees a small amount of food at a time. It works, but then you have to clean it afterward, so it is usually more work than mashing food with a fork.

Other than traditional baby food in a jar, there are all sorts of special baby foods and snacks. Most are expensive, and all are optional. Some may occasionally be worth buying for the entertainment value, or for the baby to work on fine motor skills with.

The longer you can delay the baby's introduction to sugar, the better it will be for their teeth and their overall health.

Most of the small objects that children choke on these days are food: grapes, hot dogs, nuts. Be careful what you are feeding your child, and how.

## *High chair*

Around five or six months, your baby will be able to sit up in the high chair. The basic requirements are that it must:

- Put the baby at a convenient height for eating at or next to the table (measure your table height).
- Keep the baby from falling out.
- Not tip over.
- Be sturdy, because older toddlers will try to climb all over it.
- Be washable.

If it has a tray, ideally the tray should be easily removable with only one hand, and easily washable. The writers of *Baby Bargains* noted that some dishwasher-safe trays are actually too big to go into a dishwasher.

Older highchairs have fewer safety features, and can be startlingly easy for a baby to slide out of.

### The sippy cup, and baby dinnerware

I am not a big fan of sippy cups. They tend to gravitate toward odd corners, where they lurk and hide, until given away by the odor of fermenting milk. They are hard to clean properly. They teach toddlers that they can be careless with their cups, and throw them all over the place without spilling anything or breaking the cup.

Be careful what you are teaching your child about reality: give them a spillable, and perhaps breakable, cup right from the start—under supervision. (But not *too* breakable; skip the glass cups if you have hard tile or stone floors.) We use small glass juice cups. Our daughter could drink from a straw by the age of ten months. She quickly learned that she has to be careful not to spill (though she still frequently does spill, and we frequently have to remind her to be careful, and model how to be careful). She doesn't break plates or cups any more often than I do—she is short, and most things that she drops don't have far to fall to the floor. Barbara Curtis has talked about this in her books: giving children things they need to be careful with, and then yourself modeling how to be careful with things.

Baby spoons are nice to have, but are not absolutely necessary—a regular teaspoon will do fine.

## Sleep

The textbook baby does not exist; little babies go through stages very fast, but still at their own pace. Their sleep patterns and needs will change over time; what works to get them to sleep one week might not work the next. Even so-called "good sleepers" will go through phases of teething or other development where they simply do not sleep all that well. According to Barbara Curtis, in *The Mommy Survival Guide,* the best thing to do is to let go of your expectation of eight hours of sleep for you (and of any set number of hours of sleep for your baby). Then, when either of you gets a full night's sleep, it is a bonus.

After a while, you will get a good sense of when the baby is tired and ready to sleep. Sleep harmonization as a breastfeeding mother is a wonderful thing; nursing the baby to sleep releases hormones that help you to go to sleep.

Elizabeth Pantley, in *The No-Cry Sleep Solution*, recommends detaching the baby from the breast just as, or just before, they fall asleep.

## *Toys*

Keep toys few and timeless, and continue to resist the invasion of the stuffed animals. For the rest, let the baby play with safe household objects, like small pots and pans (which they generally prefer to toys, anyway).

## *Clothes*

Your child will have outgrown three or four sizes of baby clothes by the end of the first year. There is some hope of catching up on organizing baby clothes when your child gets up in the 2T and 3T sizes (where they will stay for a while).

## *Books and television*

Have fun reading all of your old childhood favorites to your baby. Most babies have only a short attention span for books, unless they are chewing on them and ripping them up. It's best to only give them books that are in good condition—books with ripped pages and covers invite babies to tear right in.

Postpone their introduction to television as long as you can. The fewer licensed characters that they can recognize, the easier your shopping trips with them will be. If you need encouragement in this, go to *Charlie and the Chocolate Factory*, and re-read the Oompa-Loompa's diatribe against "That nauseating, foul, unclean/Repulsive television screen", which recommended throwing away the TV, and replacing it with a "lovely bookshelf on the wall". Sometimes, though, television is the only way that a busy mother can get a break. If you must, videos are better than advertising-laden TV programs. Children love repetition, and are willing to watch the same few videos over and over.

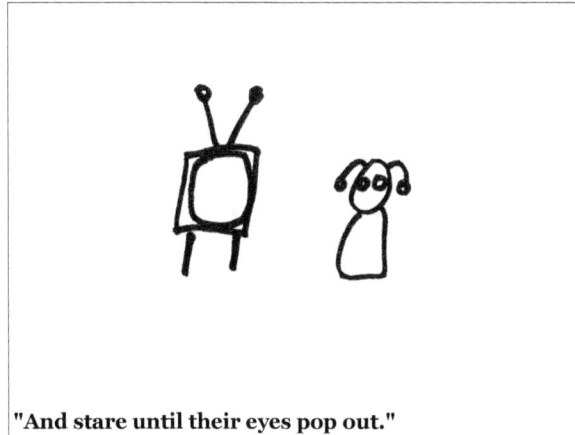

**"And stare until their eyes pop out."**

# *Travel*

Our rule has been to delay long trips until the baby is able to use their hands enough to play with toys and amuse themselves for a while in the car seat. But if you wait too long, the baby will start teething and be miserable anyway.

For car trips, plan on going slowly, and on making lots and lots of stops. Allow even more extra time on top of that. Some parents pack the car the night before, and throw the children into it at some ungodly hour of the morning, so they can drive a few hours before breakfast. My family is doing well to pull out of the driveway before the crack of noon.

Flying is a very family-unfriendly way to travel these days. You have the option of holding your baby on your lap, or of buying the baby a ticket and taking their car seat along to strap into the airplane seat (a seat where the car seat won't block anyone in), as long as the car seat isn't too wide to fit in the airplane seat. You may need to ask for a seat belt extender; airplane seat belts are rather short. Since flying is much safer than traveling by car or by bus, the purpose of the car seat in an airplane is more to keep the baby from roaming than to protect them in a crash. Most babies are accustomed to sleeping in their car seats for a while.

The changing air pressure on takeoff and landing are painful for babies; let them nurse or suck on a pacifier to ease the pressure on their eardrums.

It is possible to rent car seats at car rental agencies, along with renting a car, but you don't know exactly what they are going to give you until you get there. It might be better to rent from a baby equipment rental company at your destination, if you can coordinate things so that you have the car seat when you need it.

Likewise, you don't know what you're going to get with a hotel crib until you see it.[145]

## *Health*

These are the germ-laden places that I blame the majority of our illnesses on:

- Doctor's office
- Church nursery[146]
- Shopping carts
- Restaurant high chairs
- "Toddler traps" (play areas at the malls, stores, museums, etc.)

If we used daycare or rental strollers, these would be on the list, too.

Hand sanitizer and even handwashing are next to useless when your baby puts everything, including their grubby hands, straight into their mouth. Carrying your baby in a baby carrier in these places can keep them out of contact with many obnoxious germs, and remarkably healthier. Let them play in the dirt instead. (Very few of the bacteria present in dirt are ones that can make the baby sick.) Fresh air and sunshine will do you both good.

---

145 See the CPSC "Hotel and Motel Crib and Play Yard Safety Checklist" at **http://www.cpsc.gov/cpscpub/pubs/5136.html**

146 Which is another place you may find baby equipment and toys that are horrifyingly out of step with modern safety standards.

# *Health care*

Your baby will probably have many well-baby visits during their first year. Check ahead of time to see if these are covered by your baby's health insurance—some states require insurance coverage for these by law.

## *Growth*

At every visit, the baby's growth will be assessed. Breastfed babies have a different growth trajectory from formula-fed babies: they grow very fast in the first six months, then level off more sharply, so it is better to use the World Health Organization growth charts[147] to assess growth, if breastfeeding.

Remember that growth charts reflect the growth of healthy babies, and that some healthy babies will naturally be at one extreme or the other. Growth charts are a little misleading, because they show growth as a smooth process. Babies tend to grow piece-wise, in little jumps, spurts, and plateaus; sometimes shooting up in length, sometimes gaining bulk in width.

## *Development*

The doctor will also assess how the baby is meeting developmental milestones. Don't be too worried if your baby seems a little slow: the range of normal development is very, very wide. A child that walks at eight months is fairly normal, and so is a child that doesn't walk until fifteen months.

## *Vaccines*

The main purpose for well-child visits is to vaccinate the baby. Probably vaccines are covered by your baby's health insurance, or by some state or federal program, although you should of course check ahead of time (vaccines are very expensive if you pay for them out of pocket). The current vaccine schedule is long, and contains many vaccines that you and I probably never received. The doctor's office will have an up-to-date copy

---

147 Growth charts for breastfed boys and girls are available at
**http://www.who.int/childgrowth/standards/en/**

of the vaccination schedule. You can also find them through your state health department, and through the Centers for Disease Control and Prevention (CDC).[148]

You should receive a Vaccine Information Statement for nearly all of the vaccines that your baby will receive, before the vaccinations are given, telling you what the vaccine is for, and the risks of the vaccine—this is required by federal law. If necessary, you can get them from the Centers for Disease Control website.[149] If you think your child was harmed by a vaccine, *stop giving the child that vaccine*, and report it to the Vaccine Adverse Event Reporting System (VAERS). For severe cases, you may be able to make a petition and collect damages from the National Vaccine Injury Compensation Program (NVICP; the vaccine manufacturers are immune by law from litigation). There have been about 200 petitions made per year in recent years.[150] To date, all petitions regarding vaccine-induced autism have been dismissed. In the twenty years of the program, nearly $1.8 billion have been awarded for some 2,200 or so petitions (the NVICP generally also pays attorneys' fees, even if the claim is dismissed).

You can see from the NVICP payouts that vaccines are admitted to be not *entirely* safe. The vaccine debate is a whole big can of worms, and both sides have strong arguments. On the one hand, many diseases can be prevented or reduced in severity with vaccinations. On the other hand, vaccinations carry risks, not all of which are known to science at this time. My scientific opinion (though I am not a doctor) is that the side-effects of vaccines are very probably under-reported and under-estimated, because of the medical paradigm (and bias) that "Vaccines are great, they prevent disease!" and also because of simple duncery like "This couldn't be Disease X, they've been vaccinated for it!". The benefits of vaccines are probably overstated as well. Likewise, probably some of the anecdotal evidence for vaccine damage is a result of an anti-technological bias: "If it's artificial, then it can't be good for you!", and of sheer coincidence—my son was very fussy and had a fever for a couple of days after his last doctor visit. But I know it wasn't

---

148 Find links to vaccination schedules at
**http://www.cdc.gov/vaccines/recs/schedules/default.htm**
149 Find Vaccine Information Statements at
**http://www.cdc.gov/vaccines/pubs/vis/default.htm**
150 See the NVICP Statistics Report at
**http://www.hrsa.gov/vaccinecompensation/statistics_report.htm**

from the shots, because he didn't get any. If he had gotten some vaccinations at that visit, I would have blamed the shots. Also, there may be a few lawyers circulating vaccination horror stories in hopes of drumming up some more NVICP work (remember that they get paid whether the petition is granted or dismissed).

My preference is to do some vaccinations, and skip others, depending on risk versus benefit. I am not a fan of the combination vaccines, or multiple shots given at one time, because if there is a severe reaction, you don't know which one caused the reaction, so you have to stop them all. The CDC website has lots of information on vaccine risks and benefits, though I must say that you will get much better information there by reading the pages targeted toward medical professionals, rather than the watered-down low-reading-level pablum that they have put together for parents. Remember, too, that the CDC advocates strongly in favor of vaccinations, despite the known risks.

In any case, if your baby has known allergies, these need to be mentioned before every vaccination. Vaccinating babies with things that they are allergic to is never recommended!

Even for the vaccines the baby receives, they won't necessarily develop immunity to those diseases; most vaccines have effectiveness rates of 80% to 95%.[151] Also, some vaccines won't build up the baby's immunity sufficiently until the danger period for the disease has already passed. In these cases the vaccine is more for the benefit of the baby's siblings, friends, and relatives.

Then there are the issues of vaccine shedding, and of getting sick from the vaccine itself. Children that receive live-virus vaccines can shed the virus in their stool and bodily fluids, and infect others. In the U.S., the last "wild" case of paralytic polio was in 1979—thirty years ago; from 1980 to 1999, 144 of the 152 reported cases of polio were caused by the vaccine itself (the live-virus version—phased out in 2000); the other eight cases were imported.[152] Currently the MMR (measles, mumps, and rubella) and varicella (chicken pox) vaccines contain live viruses.[153] The annual flu vaccine, in the nasal mist form, does as well.

---

151 See the Questions and Answers link for each vaccine at the CDC website.

152 See the polio vaccine FAQ at **http://www.cdc.gov/vaccines/vpd-vac/polio/dis-faqs.htm**

Some doctors and pediatricians are dropping patients who refuse to be vaccinated according to the recommended schedule, or pressuring them to sign "Yes, I'm a bad parent for not vaccinating my child" forms; yet another factor to consider.

## Sign language

It takes a long time for babies to acquire any words or language. But they are able to learn some simple sign language much earlier than they can talk. Learning even a few signs will make it much easier for your baby to communicate with you.[154] "Milk", "more," "all done", and "sleep" are good ones. Whether you want to learn "real" sign language, or just make up your own signs, is up to you. Most baby sign language books we looked at seemed overwhelming and overambitious to us. We found a book that demonstrated a few basic American Sign Language signs, in a format that made it easy for both child and parent to learn.[155] We started reading the book with our baby when she was about six months old. She ended up learning five or six signs.

## Fertility returns

Sooner or later, you will be fertile again. No doubt you got the "so what birth control are you going to use?" question from your health care provider soon after the baby was born. Some people (including me) prefer not to have their hormones meddled with. Natural family planning/fertility awareness and the lactational amenorrhea method are undoubtedly the most frugal, least physically intrusive, and most empowering methods of avoiding pregnancy. Or you could just choose "none of above", and let the next pregnancy come when it may.

## Paying the birth bills

The worlds of health care billing and health insurance not only have their own languages, they also have their own time scales. Months after the birth, you can still be

---

153 See the first answer in the MMR FAQ at **http://www.cdc.gov/vaccines/vpd-vac/combo-vaccines/mmr/faqs-mmr-hcp.htm**

154 See **http://www.babysignlanguage.com/** for a great deal more about baby sign language.

155 *Let's Sign!: Every Baby's Guide to Communicating with Grownups*, by Kelly Ault.

receiving practically incomprehensible statements, and bills, and what-have-you. Don't panic. It's possible, and often profitable, to dispute billing issues with the hospital, and to appeal claims issues with the insurer.

# *First haircut*

In the beginning, the baby's head grows as fast as their hair, and then probably most of the hair will fall out. As cute as it might be to let it grow after that, probably your baby will end up getting a haircut sooner or later. It will probably be easier on the baby and on you to be frugal, and cut their hair yourself. It is easy to do, as long as you aren't too fussy about the results. Remember: You get better at the things you do.

The trick is to only do a few snips at a time. Give them a series of little haircuts, spread out over several hours or several days, rather than one big haircut. Use blunt-pointed (but still sharp) scissors, to avoid poking the baby if they are wiggly. Wavy or curly hair is more forgiving of imprecise cutting than straight hair is.

The simplest cut is to gather a small section of hair in your fingers, and then snip the whole section at once. Maybe let the baby play with the hair you just cut off. Repeat on the other side. Now, give your baby a break so they don't get bored or angry. Come back later and do a little more.

For later, when your baby has more hair, I will tell you the basics of hair cutting. There are only a few major variables in haircutting:

- How the hair on the head is divided up into sections.

- What angle (relative to the surface of the head) the hair of a particular section is held at to be cut: straight down for a very blunt cut line, at higher angles for a softer and more layered line, with straight up being the most layered (think of how the hair will lie on the head when it is released).

- How short to cut the section. Cut a reference swath first, then cut the rest of the section to match.

- Whether or not you want to blend the sections into each other, or leave them distinct.

# *Family rituals*

I usually think of rituals as being religious observances or ceremonial occasions, but Alexandra Stoddard has made me think of them as part of everyday life. She said, in *Living a Beautiful Life*, that rituals soothe by "making daily tasks into times of enrichment through planning and special personal details..."[156] She emphasizes choosing personal details that engage all of the senses.

So, to make a diaper changing ritual, you might have a pretty mat to lay the baby on, something visually interesting nearby for you and the baby to look at, sweet-smelling soap for washing your hands afterwards, and maybe a special diaper time song to sing to the baby. Then diaper changes would be less of a chore, and would incorporate more elements of delight.

The details that you include in your rituals need not be expensive. Sometimes it is just having a certain procedure for how you do something. Other times, you can find items that are used, but still beautiful. Or you can make your own, such as having a family ritual of making a Christmas ornament as a family, and slowly accumulate a collection over the years.

Some contexts you might consider creating family rituals for:

- Mealtimes
- Bathtime
- Bedtime
- Special songs and games
- Family worship/devotional times
- Weekly structure of activities
- Holidays
- Vacations
- Birthdays

Before long, you will have a family culture that incorporates and blends elements from both of the parents' families, and that builds on them in a unique way.

---

156 Page 3.

Rituals can support frugality by being an investment of thought and care. It takes some extra effort to create a ritual, but less effort afterward to maintain it. Earlier in the book, I mentioned having a bill-paying ritual: a regular time and a well-equipped place to sit down and pay the bills. Once you get the ritual set up, the activity is much easier, because you don't have to think about it as much. Everything you need is right there. When I stopped using disposable diapers, cloth diapering became much easier, because I didn't have to decide which kind of diaper to use at every diaper change. Recently, I gave up using the dishwasher (as a personal challenge), and created an evening dishwashing ritual. Suddenly, handwashing dishes became much less of a chore. I have a weekly cleaning routine posted on my refrigerator, that saves me from having to think too hard about what to do next.

From these experiences, it is clear to me that much of my exhaustion comes from having too many choices to make. (An observation that Barbara Curtis, in *The Mommy Survival* Guide, has also made, as has Deborah Shaw Lewis in *Motherhood Stress*.) Rituals can reduce the number of choices to a more manageable level.

## *Babysitters*

Finding a good babysitter that is available when you need them is always a chore. It seems like anyone who has time to babysit is either too old to chase a baby around, or too young to be left in charge. Everyone else seems overscheduled with school, work, and other activities.

Try asking family, friends, neighbors, co-workers, or their teenaged children. Otherwise, hire a college student, or a random adult that is advertising and looking for babysitting work (check their references carefully). Or start a babysitting co-op with other parents (a lot of work, but some parents have successfully organized them).

Truthfully, we have only very rarely used a babysitter for our two children. When I am breastfeeding a child every couple of hours, and I adamantly refuse to pump or to use formula, I can't leave them with anyone for very long. So we either stay home (too tired to go anywhere), or we take them along with us. Then they have a chance to see the world a little, and to learn how to behave in public. Our culture is very age-segregated, many young children go straight from home to daycare, then back to home, dinner, bath, and bed. Often people have been pleasantly surprised to meet our daughter out and about, behaving well and not tearing up the place (much).

The main exception, where we did hire a babysitter, was for the birth of our second child. Then we needed someone to be available on rather short notice to care for our toddler. We ended up hiring a doula, since doulas are used to being around births, and to being called in at odd hours. It worked out well. The other exception was jury duty, where we hired a college student on break.

As Rebecca Prewett once heard from an older, more experienced mother,[157] the more time that we spend with our children, the more grace we receive, and the more opportunities that we have to teach and train them to behave well.

## *Mom support*

As Susan Strasser noted in *Never Done*, the movement of women's work out of the home into highly structured workplaces, and the movement of social life into public areas (such as restaurants and theaters) that are inhospitable to small children, has had an enormously isolating effect on mothers who do stay at home to care for children. I don't know of *any* other stay-at-home moms in the apartment complex where I live.

Likewise, most women these days have received absolutely inadequate training to be mothers and household managers, as Deborah Shaw Lewis noted in *Motherhood Stress*. In the book, she delved into the many, varied stresses of motherhood, which include unpredictability, lack of control, complexity, lack of feedback and status, unwanted and often conflicting advice, and a plethora of choices at every turn.

If you are interested in finding some moms' support in your area, the first place you should look is at the church you attend, if you have one. Decide whether you are looking for a group of peers—other mothers of young children—or for more of a mentoring relationship with older mothers. Also decide whether you are looking for one or two close friends, or a larger mom group. You may want to check your local ads for groups advertising their meetings.

---

157 In her online article "Mommy Burnout" at **http://www.fix.net/~rprewett/burnout.html** [Site unavailable, unfortunately—Dec. 2010]

National organizations such as MOMS, MOPS, and La Leche League have websites that can help you find the local chapter meeting nearest to you. Some groups you can attend for no cost, and others have fees. Or you could start an informal group with your family and friends.

I have not been part of any group of this sort myself, beyond an odd meeting or two; it is difficult to show up at a scheduled time with small children, and to work around nap times. Also, I have been reluctant to leave nursing infants or preverbal toddlers in child-care, when that is provided. (La Leche League encourages mothers to keep their young children with them.)

## *Saving for college*

As much as you would like to get started on your baby's college fund, it is smarter to get yourself out of debt first, and then to save for your retirement. Your child will be able to get student loans for school, they hand them out like candy, but you will not be able to get loans to live on when you are retired.

Once you have a good start on saving for retirement, then start saving up for your child's future...which may or may not include college. Money to go to a trade school, or to start up a business, might be more useful to them than a college education. So I think that college saving plans, such as state 529 plans, may not be the best choice; they have some tax advantages, but you sacrifice a great deal of future flexibility.

## *The first birthday*

The first year of a child's life goes by very fast. They start out as a helpless newborn, and by the end of the first year, they are constantly on the go.

How frugal you can be with the first birthday party varies—some people have only a very small celebration; in other families, it is a huge gathering of family and friends. Personally, we try to keep the first birthday party modest—there is plenty of time for birthday party inflation later. One rule of thumb is one birthday party guest per year of the child's age. We keep the birthday presents modest, too—I think an attractive box would be the perfect present for a one-year-old.[158] (Anything inside the box would be a bonus.)

In any case, I hope that this book has helped equip you to get to your baby's first birthday more frugally, and more joyfully.

---

158 Skip the wrapping paper; if you own books, you will not want to encourage them to rip up paper, until they are old enough to know the difference.

# Acknowledgments

My husband deserves many thanks, for invaluable advice and help with the illustrations, cover, and editing, and for making space in our busy family life for me to work on this book.

Many thanks too, to the experts, both expert and amateur, who generously wrote down their words of wisdom in books and blogs and web pages, from whom I have learned pretty much everything that I know. I gave attribution where I could.

I used several free software tools to write this book. The book outline was developed in FreeMind. The book was written in OpenOffice Writer. The illustrations, as you probably guessed, are Sharpie marker on white paper, photographed by my husband (because he couldn't find his scanner cord). I put the cover together in Inkscape. The foofy font is Little Lord Fontleroy.

# Appendix: Creative Problem-Solving in Frugality

Tightwaddery without creativity is deprivation.

—Amy Dacyczyn, *The Complete Tightwad Gazette*

In their engineering textbook *Creative Problem Solving: Thinking Skills for a Changing World,* Edward and Monika Lumsdaine note that homemakers are among the most creative people—by necessity, because of the variety of problems that they face every day, and the challenges of making do with what is on hand.

Creativity-nurturing books like *The Artist's Way* may be helpful in unlocking your creative brain, although many of these do seem to have a bias toward the more academic arts such as writing, painting, drawing, music, and dance. But solving your household problems can be a creative work in its own right, and a great source of personal satisfaction.

Despite the low status afforded to them, frugal homemaking and childrearing require strong creative thinking skills, and not a small amount of mental agility, to creatively connect household needs to available resources. I can tell you tricks that work in my situation, and show you examples of my thought processes, but your skills and resources are likely to be different from mine, and what works for me may not work for you.

The first, and often unrecognized, step in creativity is to take in lots of information for your brain to absorb. Reading, learning, exploring, play—things that look like "goofing off", but actually aren't. (Declutter your brain first, to make room for all this stuff, by writing down, on paper or in some electronic form, all the things that your brain is trying to remember for you.)

Then, when you have a problem to solve, you have material to draw on. For example, say that I run out of disposable diapers. I have cloth diapers around as a backup, so that's no big deal—I'll just need to wash them later. But if I ran out of cloth diapers, what would I do?

Well, what are the essential requirements for a diaper? I know that it has to be absorbent, to soak up urine, and it has to keep poop from running out. It has to be soft on the baby's skin, and not be a hazard to the baby. I need to be able to affix it to the baby, and remove it later. It needs to be small enough to not hamper the baby's movements. Probably there needs to be some sort of cover over the absorbent part.

Now, what do I have in my home that would fit those requirements? If I brainstorm for a minute, I come up with: Receiving blankets, if I fold them to fit around the baby. Old T-shirts. Hand towels. Scrap fabric for sewing, including some flannel. Old sheets that I could cut up. Pillowcases. (That is the advantage of shopping at thrift stores and rummage sales: easy come, easy go.) I could take an old onesie and put a folded washcloth inside it.

Granted, most of these would make inferior diapers, but that's a lot of options. I could probably diaper the baby for a week on my husband's old T-shirts alone. (Not that he would approve of it.)

Next comes an evaluation step: given my options, which would be the best to start with? Probably receiving blankets, since they are very close to being flat diapers anyway. I know, from things I've read, more or less how to fold a flat diaper into a triangle, and how to pin it on the baby.

The next thing, is what to use for a diaper cover (assuming that I'm out of diaper covers too)? I could skip the cover in this case, since the receiving blanket diaper is bulky by itself, and will cover the baby fairly well. Or I could put a pair of baby pants on the baby, and change everything when it got wet. That should buy me enough time to go out and buy diapers, or to wash and dry a load of diapers.

Then, the implementation step: diaper the baby with a receiving blanket. Is that good enough? Does it need improvement? (I have tried it, and it worked. It is more bulky than a prefold diaper, though, and takes up more room in the diaper pail. I have also tried the "stuffed onesie" diaper, and that worked fairly well, too.)

One of Alexandra Stoddard's books is called *Open Your Eyes*—the main idea is that you need to be able to really stop and see things, before you can effectively decorate your home. There's a similar process in creative frugality: you need to be able to see clearly just what is needed to solve your problem, and just what resources you have that you might use to do it.

Another of her sayings about creativity (in this case creativity in decorating) is: "To putter is to discover."[159] Also:

> The smallest gem of an idea can turn into a real jewel, and puttering allows you time and space to develop your concept.

It is not just the little problems that require creative problem-solving; the big ones do too. Implementing bigger solutions requires discipline and perseverance, as well as enthusiasm. Being creative does seem to take an awful lot of energy sometimes. If you're feeling drained, take a rest from it, and goof off for a while. Downtime is just as important as up time; this is one of the secrets of the highest achievers.

---

159 In *Living a Beautiful Life*, page 29.

# Resources

## *Print Resources*

Christopher Alexander, Kara Ishikawa, and Murray Silverstein, with Max Jacobsen, Ingrid Fiksdahl-King, and Shlomo Angel, *A Pattern Language: Towns, Buildings, Construction.* Oxford University Press, 1977.

Kelly Ault and Leo Landry (illus.), *Let's Sign!: Every Baby's Guide to Communicating with Grownups.* Boston, MA: Houghton Mifflin Co., 2005.

Robert Bradley, *Husband-Coached Childbirth.* [Now in its fifth edition; I'm not sure which of the earlier editions is the one that I read.] For the fifth edition: co-authors Marjie Hathaway, Jay Hathaway, and James Hathaway. New York, NY: Bantam Dell, 2008.

Jim and Sally Conway, *Women in Midlife Crisis.* Wheaton, IL: Tyndale House Publishers, Inc., 1997.

Barbara Curtis, *The Mommy Survival Guide: Making the Most of the Mommy Years.* Kansas City, MO: Beacon Hill Press of Kansas City, 2006.

Amy Dacyczyn, *The Complete Tightwad Gazette: Promoting Thrift as a Viable Alternative Lifestyle.* New York, NY: Villard Books, 1998.

Roald Dahl, *Charlie and the Chocolate Factory.* New York, NY: Bantam Books, 1979.

Marva Dawn, *Keeping the Sabbath Wholly.* Grand Rapids, MI: William B. Eerdmans Publishing Company, 1989.

Barbara Deckert, *Sewing for Plus Sizes: Creating Clothes that Fit and Flatter*. Newtown, CT: The Taunton Press, 2002.

Grantly Dick-Read, *Childbirth without Fear: The Principles and Practice of Natural Childbirth*. London: Pinter & Martin, Ltd, 2005

Denise Fields, *Baby Bargains, 8th edition: Secrets to Saving 20% to 50% on Baby Furniture, Gear, Clothes, Toys, Maternity Wear, and Much, Much More!* Boulder, CO: Windsor Peak Press, 2009.

Henci Goer, *A Thinking Woman's Guide to a Better Birth*. New York, NY: Berkeley Pub. Group, 1999.

Brady E. Hamilton, Joyce E. Martin, and Stephanie J. Ventura, "Birth: Preliminary Data for 2007". National Vital Statistics Reports **57** 12, March 18, 2008. Available online at **http://www.cdc.gov/nchs/data/nvsr/nvsr57/nvsr57_12.pdf**

Shannon Hayes, *Radical Homemakers: Reclaiming Domesticity from a Consumer Culture*. Richmondville, NY: Left to Write Press, 2010.

Karl H. E. Kroemer, *'Extra-Ordinary Ergonomics': How to accommodate Small and Big Persons, The Disabled and Elderly, Expectant Mothers, and Children*. Boca Raton, FL: CRC Press, 2006.

La Leche League International, *The Womanly Art of Breastfeeding, Seventh Edition*. New York, NY: Penguin Group, 2004.

Don Lancaster, *The Incredible Secret Money Machine*. Howard W Sams and Co., Inc., 1979.

Deborah Shaw Lewis, *Motherhood Stress: Finding Encouragement in the Ultimate Helping Profession*. Dallas, TX: Word Publishing, 1989.

Jean Liedloff, *The Continuum Concept: Allowing Human Nature to Work Successfully*. Reading, MA: Addison-Wesley Publishing Company, Inc., 1977.

Mark Lino and Andrea Carlson, "Expenditures on Children by Families, 2008". U.S. Department of Agriculture, Center for Nutrition Policy and Promotion, Miscellaneous Publication No. 1528-2008. July 2009. Available online at **http://www.cnpp.usda.gov/Publications/CRC/crc2008.pdf**

Edward Lumsdaine and Monika Lumsdaine, *Creative Problem Solving: Thinking Skills for a Changing World*. New York, NY: McGraw-Hill, Inc., 1995.

Elizabeth Pantley, *The No-Cry Sleep Solution: Gentle Ways to Help Your Baby Sleep Through The Night*. Chicago, IL: Contemporary Books, 2002.

Martin Poriss, *How to Live Cheap But Good*. Dell, 1974.

Dave Ramsey, *The Total Money Makeover: A Proven Plan for Financial Fitness*. Nashville, TN: Nelson Books, 2007.

J.D. Roth, *Your Money: The Missing Manual*. Sebastopol, CA: O'Reilly Media, Inc., 2010.

Janet Schwegel (ed.), Pam England (foreword), *et al.*, *Adventures in Natural Childbirth: Tales from Women on the Joys, Fears, Pleasures, and Pains of Giving Birth Naturally*. New York, NY: Avalon Publishing Group, Inc., 2005.

William Sears and Martha Sears, *The Baby Book: Everything You Need to Know About Your Baby from Birth to Age Two*. Boston, MA: Little, Brown and Company, 1993.

William Sears and Martha Sears, with Linda Hughey Holt, *The Pregnancy Book: Month-by-Month, Everything You Need to Know From America's Baby Experts*. New York, NY: Little, Brown, and Company, 1997.

Amanda Blake Soule, *Handmade Home: Simple Ways to Repurpose Old Materials into New Family Treasures*. Boston, MA: Trumpeter Books, 2009. Contains directions for making cloth prefold diapers, and baby slings.

Thomas Sowell, *Basic Economics: A Citizen's Guide to the Economy*. New York, NY: Basic Books, 2000.

Alexandra Stoddard, *The Decoration of Houses*. New York, NY: Avon Books, 1997.

Alexandra Stoddard, *Living a Beautiful Life: 500 Ways to Add Elegance, Order, Beauty and Joy to Every Day of Your Life*. New York, NY: Avon Books, 1986.

Alexandra Stoddard, *Living Beautifully Together*. New York, NY: Doubleday, 1989.

Alexandra Stoddard, *Open Your Eyes*. New York, NY: William Morrow and Company, 1998.

Susan Strasser, *Never Done: A History of American Housework*. New York, NY: Pantheon Books, 1982.

John Townsend, *Hiding From Love: How to Change the Withdrawal Patterns That Isolate and Imprison You*. Colorado Springs, CO: NavPress, 1991.

Ingrid Trobisch, *The Joy of Being a Woman...And What a Man Can Do*. San Francisco, CA: Harper & Row, Publishers, 1975.

Gwen Weising, *Finding Dollars for Family Fun: Creating Happy Memories on a Budget*. Grand Rapids, MI: Fleming H. Revell, 1993.

## *Internet Resources (as of December 2010)*

American Association of Pediatrics Practice Guidelines for hyperbilirubinemia (jaundice) in newborns:

http://aappolicy.aappublications.org/cgi/content/full/pediatrics%3B114/1/297

American College of Nurse-Midwives: **http://www.midwife.org/**

Baby sign language: **http://www.babysignlanguage.com/**

Car buying tips: **http://www.carbuyingtips.com/**

Car-Seat.org: **http://www.car-seat.org/**

Centers for Disease Control and Prevention vaccine information:
**http://www.cdc.gov/vaccines/default.htm**

Childbirth Connection (improving maternity care): **http://www.childbirthconnection.org/**

Citizens' Council on Health Freedom (genetic privacy and other health care issues):
**http://www.cchconline.org/index.php3**

Citizens' Council on Health Freedom (formerly Citizens' Council on Health Care) chart of state's newborn blood sample retention policies (how long states keep blood samples from newborn screenings): **http://www.cchconline.org/pdf/50_States-Newborn_Blood_Retention_Policies_FINAL.pdf**

Coalition for Improving Maternity Services (CIMS) Mother-Friendly Childbirth Initiative:
**http://www.motherfriendly.org/pdf/MFCI_english.pdf**

Consumer Product Safety Commission: **http://www.cpsc.gov/**

Consumer Product Safety Commission, "Hotel and Motel Crib and Play Yard Safety Checklist":
**http://www.cpsc.gov/cpscpub/pubs/5136.html**

Consumer Product Safety Commission, "Used child safety seat checklist":

**http://www.cpsafety.com/articles/UsedSeat.aspx**

Consumer Reports (some content cannot be viewed without a subscription):

**http://www.consumerreports.org/**

Cost of Raising a Child Calculator, USDA: **http://www.cnpp.usda.gov/calculatorintro.htm**

Craigslist: **http://craigslist.org/**

Dave Ramsey (getting out of debt): **http://www.daveramsey.com/**

The Diaper Hyena (links to free cloth diaper patterns and diapers for sale from work-at-home-moms): **http://www.thediaperhyena.com/reap.htm** [site unavailable as of December 2010 , unfortunately]

DONA International (doula association): **http://www.dona.org/**

"Effects of Hospital Economics on Maternity Care" article by Susan Hodges and Henci Goer: **http://www.yourbody-yourbirth.com/uploads/maternitycareandhospitaleconomics.pdf**

"Expenditures on Children by Families 2007" report by Mark Lino, for the U.S. Department of Agriculture Center for Nutrition Policy and Promotion:

**http://www.cnpp.usda.gov/Publications/CRC/crc2007.pdf**

"Expenditures on Children by Families 2008" report by Mark Lino and Andrea Carlson, for the U.S. Department of Agriculture Center for Nutrition Policy and Promotion:

**http://www.cnpp.usda.gov/Publications/CRC/crc2008.pdf**

"Expenditures on Children by Families 2009" report by Mark Lino, for the U.S. Department of Agriculture Center for Nutrition Policy and Promotion:

**http://www.cnpp.usda.gov/Publications/CRC/crc2009.pdf**

Ezzo.info (criticism of the *Babywise* and *Preparation for Parenting* books):
**http://www.ezzo.info/**

The Family Corner (articles on Christian parenting): **http://www.fix.net/~rprewett/** [Site unavailable as of December 2010]

Family Friendly Jury Duty (advocates for jury duty exemptions for caregivers):
**http://www.familyfriendlyjuryduty.org/**

FreeCycle: **http://www.freecycle.org/**

The Frugal Baby (not affliated with the author of this book): **http://www.thefrugalbaby.com/**

GentleBirth midwife archives: **http://www.gentlebirth.org/archives/**

Gentle Christian Mothers (parenting articles and links to resources):
**http://www.gentlechristianmothers.com/** [Site unavailable as of December 2010]

Health Care and Education Reconciliation Act of 2010: full text available from the Library of Congress via:
**http://thomas.loc.gov/**

ICAN database of hospitals with VBAC bans: **http://www.ican-online.org/vbac-ban-info**

Internal Revenue Service "Alternative Minimum Tax Assistant for Individuals":
**http://www.irs.gov/businesses/small/article/0,,id=150703,00.html**

Internal Revenue Service information on childcare tax credit, IRS Publication 503, "Child and Dependent Care Expenses":

**http://www.irs.gov/pub/irs-pdf/p503.pdf**

Internal Revenue Service information on employing in-home caregivers, IRS Publication 926, "Household Employer's Tax Guide":  **http://www.irs.gov/publications/p926/index.html**

Internal Revenue Service FSA and HSA information, IRS Publication 969, "Health Savings Accounts and Other Tax-Favored Savings Plans": **http://www.irs.gov/pub/irs-pdf/p969.pdf**

Internal Revenue Service withholding calculator can be found at:
**http://www.irs.gov/individuals/index.html**

Kellymom (information on breastfeeding and parenting): **http://kellymom.com**

La Leche International: **http://www.llli.org/**

The Mamatoto Project (babywearing tutorials and how-to's): **http://wearyourbaby.com/**

Midwives Alliance of North America: **http://mana.org/**

"Mommy Burnout" article by Rebecca Prewett:
**http://www.fix.net/~rprewett/burnout.html** [Site unavailable as of December 2010, unfortunately]

Mommylife blog by Barbara Curtis (mothering, teaching your children, politics, Downs' Syndrome): **http://mommylife.net/**

MOMS (Moms Offering Moms Support): **http://www.momsclub.org/**

MOPS (Mothers of Preschoolers): **http://www.mops.org/**

More Month Than Money e-book (frugal meal planning), from New Century Homestead:

**http://nchstd.documents.s3.amazonaws.com/More%20Month%20than%20Money %20PDF.pdf**

National Vital Statistics Reports "Birth: Preliminary Data for 2007" report:
**http://www.cdc.gov/nchs/data/nvsr/nvsr57/nvsr57_12.pdf**

Patient Protection and Affordable Care Act of 2010: full text available from the Library of Congress via:

**http://thomas.loc.gov/**

Peeonastick.com (information about home pregnancy testing):
**http://www.peeonastick.com/**

Plus-Size Pregnancy (how to avoid medical over-treatment as a plus-size mother):
**http://www.plus-size-pregnancy.org/**

U.S. Department of Agriculture Cost of Food charts:
**http://www.cnpp.usda.gov/USDAFoodCost-Home.htm**

U.S. Department of Agriculture Cost of Raising a Child calculator:
**http://www.cnpp.usda.gov/calculatorintro.htm**

Walk score: **http://www.walkscore.com/**

World Health Organization growth charts:
**http://www.who.int/childgrowth/standards/en/**

"Woman to Woman" article by Helen E. Aardsma:
**http://www.themotherscompanion.org/newsletters/womantowomansample.php**

# Index

www.ingramcontent.com/pod-product-compliance
Lightning Source LLC
LaVergne TN
LVHW081323060426
835511LV00011B/1825

9 780578 078366